BECOME AN

ENERGY ADDICT™

*Simple, Powerful Ways
to Energize Your Life*

Staff Recommended Book

JON GORDON, M.A.

LONGSTREET PRESS
Atlanta, Georgia

Published by
LONGSTREET PRESS, INC.
2974 Hardman Court
Atlanta, Georgia 30305
www.longstreetpress.net

2nd printing, 2003
ISBN: 1-56352-718-9

Printed in the United States of America

Jacket and book design by Burtch Hunter Design LLC

Since today everybody thinks you're open 24/7, increasing your energy is an important survival strategy. Read Jon Gordon's *Become an Energy Addict* and learn 100 simple, powerful strategies to increase your physical, mental and spiritual energy. Read it so you can go for it!

Ken Blanchard, coauthor of *The One Minute Manager*® and *Gung Ho!*®

If you often feel like you're out of gas, slowing down, or running on fumes, this book will help you to find the fuel to enliven your life *FOR LIFE*. Full of great tips, it's an easy, enjoyable, light, and inspiring read. Jon Gordon's mind-body approach to increasing your energy really works!

Michael Gerrish, author of *The Mind-Body Makeover Project* and
   When Working Out Isn't Working Out

Become an Energy Addict can help many athletes focus and increase their energy during times of high performance. It's been a great book for all my clients who enjoy the game of golf.

Cindy Reid, author of *Cindy Reid's Ultimate Guide to Golf for
   Women*. Director of Instruction, TPC at Sawgrass, Top 50
   Female Instructor 2003

Read this compelling book and you'll get out of bed, get dressed and wonder why you ever went to bed at all! Choose from 100 terrific strategies to gain and share energy and increase your power supply. Rid yourself of Energy Vampires, practice Zoom Focus and, I would add, have a Fierce Conversation. Jon Gordon persuades us that energy acquisition is a skill anyone can learn. Positive energy is contagious. Give yourself and others this powerful infusion.

Susan Scott, author of *Fierce Conversations, Achieving Success at
   Work and In Life—One Conversation at a Time*

Your levels of energy largely determine the quality of your life; this book shows you how to feel terrific every minute of the day!

Brian Tracy, author of *Change Your Thinking/Change Your Life*

Become an Energy Addict teaches us that we can all get so much more out of our lives. I highly recommend this book to anyone who wants to be more effective, happy and energetic.

Bruce N. Bagni, Senior Vice President, General Counsel, Blue Cross and Blue Shield of Florida

Jon Gordon's *Become an Energy Addict* helps you turn your potential energy into actual energy.

Robin Wahby, Managing Partner, New York Life

Jon Gordon's positive energy is contagious. Read this book, get addicted to positive energy, and share it with everyone you know. Someone could say this: Jon Gordon's strategies for boundless energy are right on target for those who want to live a full vibrant life on all levels of their being. Gordon is one of those unique individuals who lives what he teaches.

Susan Taylor, Ph.D., author of *The Vital Energy Program*

This is the book that people need to read right now. With so many of us needing more energy for our personal and professional lives, this clearly written, practical, and insightful book will make a powerful difference in people's lives.

Barbara Kaufman, author of *Attitude*

After reading *Become an Energy Addict* I am proud to say that I am an Energy Addict. Jon Gordon's advice is concise, pertinent, and useful immediately. Changes in your life will be dramatic and will happen "right now" using his energy boosting methods. I've been recommending his energy tips to my patients with very good results. This book will get you started and his action steps will keep you energized.

Robert Mac Murray, MD Board Certified in both Family Practice (The American Board of Family Practice) and in Psychiatry and Neurology (The American Board of Psychiatry and Neurology)

Jon is truly committed to helping others reach their full potential by tapping into their inner energy. He walks the talk! You can definitely see how very quick and simple tips have helped people change their lives. Beyond just education, I've seen employees make behavioral changes that will serve them for the long term.

Mike Cooney, Director of Human Resources, PGA Tour

Energy is an essential ingredient in building a strong body, strong mind and strong spirit. I recommend *Become an Energy Addict* to anyone looking to create more energy and build more strength in their life.

Greg Finnegn, Jacksonville Jaguars and University of Colorado Strength Coach

CONTENTS

ACKNOWLEDGEMENTS

This book is dedicated to my wife Kathryn and my precious children. You are my teachers. Thank you for teaching me to love, play, open my heart and become a real Energy Addict. Your love, patience and support made this book possible.

To my Mom and Dad, thank you for always believing in me and being there with open ears and loving hearts. I am who I am because of you.

To Longstreet Press and Scott Bard, thank you for seeing my vision and helping me live my purpose.

To my brother, David Gordon, thank you for your creative ideas.

Thank you to my Father for introducing me to yoga and healthy natural foods at an early age.

To my Grandpa Eddy, thank you for your poems, inspiration, and example of how to live a long and healthy happy life.

To my literary agent, Sheree Bykofsky, thank you for your guidance and support.

Thank you to all the people who helped me grow and share my ideas. Brian Hannafin, Ted Berkery, John Busse, Ivan Goldfarb, Richie Moran, Rick Dean, Robin Wahby, Susan Drummond, Jeff Benton, Edie Williams, Amy Waag, Rich Waag, Keith Frein, Daniel Decker, Marci Weinberg, Dave Watson, John Barry, Ray

Nealon, Keith Elzia, Matt Ray, Megan McDonough, Bob Kronmiller, Vince Bagni, Macky Weaver, Karla Swatek, Dave Donaldson, Dave Goodman, Jeffrey Harrington, Tom Carter, Becky Tokich, Tom Briones, Amy Wasserman, Elizabeth Vaeth, Tom Houck, Robert Mac Murray, MD, Susan Scott, Ken Blanchard, Michael Gerrish, Susan Taylor, Brian Tracy, Cindy Reid, Greg Finnegn, and Bruce Bagni.

INTRODUCTION

"The world belongs to the energetic."

RALPH WALDO EMERSON

If you have ever said, "I wish I had more energy" or "I just don't have the energy," then I am glad you are reading this.

As I speak to people around the country, I hear it all the time. We all wish we had more energy to meet the increasing demands of everyday life. And we all wish we had more time to do all the things on our to-do list. Many of us are overstressed, overworked and overtired. The problem is it's not getting any easier. Somehow the days are getting shorter while our to-do lists are getting longer. Our pace of life continues to get faster and the demands continue to increase. We fight through each day, battling fatigue and headaches, stress and frustration, depression and grumpiness, and back and neck problems. We attempt to fight back with caffeinated drinks and candy bars with the hope they will give us just enough energy to accomplish our tasks before we crash. But when the caffeine and sugar wear off, we are left feeling tired once again. And tomorrow it starts all over.

We need more energy and time but where do we find them? Unless Congress passes legislation for a 25-hour-day, we can't increase the amount of hours in our day.

Thankfully, there is another way. We can become an Energy Addict.

During the past year I received many e-mails and calls from people who attended my seminars or received my "energy for life" tips via my e-mail newsletters. They said they incorporated several or many of my strategies into their lives and found they had more energy, felt more motivated and improved their lives significantly.

Consider Susan, who made a commitment to eat breakfast, exercise, and spend more quality time with her daughter. She is 20 pounds lighter, feels more productive at work, and now takes meaningful after-dinner walks with her daughter. They get fit together and they bond together. Or consider Vince, who wanted to become better at focusing his energy to increase his sales. Vince's sales are up 30 percent this year because he learned how to tune out distractions and get rid of the energy vampires in his life.

Or consider Amy, who now exercises in the morning and has more energy during the day. Michael now drinks water instead of diet soda, and feels the difference every day. Brian drinks Green Tea in the afternoon instead of coffee and doesn't crash any more. And Erin is much happier since she decided to invest her energy where it matters most.

Each success story made me more inclined to share my program with as many people as possible. I believe if something works, it shouldn't be kept a secret. So I decided to write this book with the hope that it reaches those who need it the most.

For many of us, our actual energy is far below our potential energy. In fact, our energy is not even a tenth of what it could be. Yet the fact that you are reading this tells me that everything is about to change. As you read each energy tip, I am confident your actual energy will rise to meet your potential energy and the results will be amazing.

My goal is that as you read this book you will think of yourself as an Energy Addict. In a world of 12-step programs that serve a great purpose and help people deal with addictions, I have a different approach. I want you to become addicted to positive energy and positive habits. As an Energy Addict, in addition to increasing your energy, you will also focus your energy on your priorities, clear out negative energy and flow with positive energy, develop a "big bang" mindset and create your life everyday through your words, thoughts, choices and actions.

Becoming an Energy Addict is more than having physical energy. We are made up of physical, mental, spiritual and emotional energy. Each area of our life contributes to our total energy. Energizing only one of your energy needs is like heating only one room in your house during the winter. Consider exercise. It may help us increase our physical and mental well being, but it will not help us clear out negative energy from a bad relationship. This negative energy can weigh us down like a ton of bricks no matter how much we exercise. It can cause us to be sluggish and tired even if we are in great shape. So to live a life filled with boundless energy we must address the energy needs of our parts and provide the fuel to energize the whole.

In this book I will share with you simple but powerful strategies that will increase your physical, mental and spiritual energy. These strategies are simple because anyone can do them. They can be started today. They are powerful because the small changes you make will produce big results. Many of my suggestions are backed by research and have proven themselves to be successful by all the people who use them. I have also personally incorporated the strategies, lessons and habits discussed in this book into my own life—and I continue to practice them every day. I need to. They have changed my life and I believe they will make a difference in yours.

I believe positive energy is contagious. My hope is the positive energy I share with you via this book will energize your life and, in turn, you will share positive energy with others. If you find that this book helps you in your life, please tell a friend. If a strategy works for you, tell your friends so they can energize their life. If you have a success story or lesson that you have learned, please share them with me. We are all teachers and students. While I teach the lessons I have learned, and discovered, I also continue to learn every day. Like you, I am living and working in new and changing times. As part of this process I hope you will share your thoughts and experiences with me as I share mine with you. Consider me your personal energy coach who is only a click away. You can reach me at Jon@JonGordon.com.

BECOME AN

ENERGY
ADDICT™

IT'S ALL ABOUT ENERGY

Everything is energy in motion.

PIR VILAYAT INAYAT KHAN

While many scientists and experts study energy, the truth is you don't have to be a scientist to know that energy is all around us and inside us. Human beings, trees, water, sunlight, air, plants and every other single thing in the universe—they're all made of energy. In fact, when we get down to it, energy is all that exists. In high school science class we learned that energy is never created nor destroyed. It is simply transformed from one form of energy to another. The energy of two cells uniting to form an embryo; a power plant turning the energy of water into electricity; a plant using the sun's energy to live; all are examples of energy flow and transformation. The same energy from sunlight that feeds an apple tree also provides us with the energy to walk, talk and think. Energy never disappears. It is recycled into other forms of energy. Energy is never stagnant. Rather, it flows, it transforms, and it creates.

While energy is a difficult concept to grasp because we can't physically see it, we can think about our everyday experiences to understand how "it's all about energy." When we eat food, we feed our bodies energy. Sunlight and water provide a plant with the energy to live. Cars need energy to drive. When we walk into a restaurant or party, we feel the energy immediately. We instantly decide whether we like the place or we don't. We might say, "That place has great energy" or "That restaurant didn't have a good feel to it."

Likewise, we meet someone we decide immediately

whether they have a "good vibe" or a "bad vibe." We read their energy and make a decision on how their energy affects us. We've all met people who have a lot of great energy. We want to be around them more. In contrast, we've also had the experience of meeting someone I call an Energy Vampire where they literally sucked the energy right out of us. If we paid close attention we could feel the energy being pulled from our bodies. Energy Vampires do exist and they will steal your energy if you let them. I will talk about them later in the book.

Energy is also found in the thoughts we think and the words we read and hear. Have you ever gotten excited about an idea and felt energized? Or listened to an energetic speaker and become motivated to take action? Or read a book and become inspired? Words are so powerful they have started fights and wars. With each book we read and each sentence we hear, we take in energy. With each thought we think we send energy to our body and project that energy out into the world.

We also find a tremendous amount of energy in music and other people. We listen to music and it lifts us up. Have you ever seen a live concert? You can literally feel the power emanating from the performer. They are sharing their energy with the audience and the audience is receiving it. The energy is so powerful you can almost touch it.

Or have you ever been in a football or baseball stadium or basketball arena? The crowd goes wild. The home team comes from behind and wins the game. It was as if they were feeding off the energy of the crowd. They were. That's why they call it "home field advantage." Or how about the way you feel after meeting an old friend for lunch or dinner. After talking to them you feel better than ever. You laughed nonstop, told stories and felt full of life. You shared energy.

Many of us also experience energy in many other ways. Have you ever said a prayer and felt God's energy fill you up? Or gone to the beach and become rejuvenated? Or hiked in the mountains and felt the energy of the trees? When you exercise do you feel like you have more energy even though you just ran two miles? When you get a good night's sleep do you feel like someone recharged your battery?

We have all of these experiences and many more like them because we are energy beings and as energy beings we interact with other forms of energy every day. We give, receive, share, transform, maximize and focus energy every day.

It's all about energy.

INCREASE
YOUR POWER SUPPLY

Too much of a good thing is wonderful.

MAE WEST

We all know someone who seems to have more energy than the rest of us. When I ask people in my seminars if they know someone who has a lot of energy, everyone in the room usually points to two or three people. We can see it with our eyes, hear it in their words and enthusiasm and feel it in their presence. Just as some people are born to play the piano or baseball better than the rest of us, there are those who, I believe, are born naturally with more energy.

However, the great news is that energy can be acquired. While we may not be born as energetic as some people, we can become more energetic by acquiring more energy. Just as a baseball player can practice hitting to improve his batting skills and an actress can practice displaying different emotions to improve her craft, all of us have the ability to become skilled at acquiring more energy.

The key is to become an Energy Addict. Like any addict who is addicted to something, an Energy Addict always wants more positive energy. Energy Addicts are always interested in increasing their power supply—acquiring more energy to become more energetic and powerful. If we measured an Energy Addict's energy supply it would far exceed that of a normal person. Energy Addicts take in more energy from more sources. They know where to find the energy—how to tap it—and how to make the most of the energy they have.

Just as a good financial planner can take your $1,000 and turn it into $5,000 while an average financial planner would turn your $1,000 into $2,000, an Energy Addict can take the same amount of energy as a normal person and create more, do more and accomplish more with it. So an Energy Addict takes in more energy and makes it work more efficiently and effectively. This leads to a larger power supply even while energy is being used every day.

And because Energy Addicts are skilled at acquiring more energy for their life, they are always replacing used energy and adding to their power supply. With all of their energy, Energy Addicts also have more to share with others. This energy can be used to help other people increase their power supply—creating a more energetic company, family, organization, neighborhood and world.

As you read on, you will discover many ways to increase your power supply. Simply remember energy acquisition is a skill. The more you do it, the better you will get. The better you get, the more you will increase your power supply. You may have not been born energetic but you can become energetic. Up to this point you may have not lived a life filled with energy, but today you can become an Energy Addict. This will allow you to create more success for yourself and others.

FIND YOUR SONG
AND PLAY THE MUSIC

Drumsound rises on the air, its throb, my heart.
A voice inside the beat says, 'I know you're tired, but come. This is the way.'

RÚMÍ

Most of us have a favorite song that lifts us up whenever we hear it. You might be sitting in your car and your favorite song will come on the radio. You start singing and before you know it your day has turned around from frustration to joy. Music is energy that vibrates just as the approximately 75 trillion cells in our body vibrate. When we hear music our bodies will often feel the music before we even realize we are moving to the beat.

Music has the power to make us laugh and cry. Think of the music from the movies "Terms of Endearment" and "Titanic." The music starts playing and the audience is reaching for tissues. Music also has the power to motivate us and inspire us. Think of the "Rocky" movies. When I hear the "Rocky" theme song I still get the urge to sprint a hundred yards.

Music sets the tone in restaurants and shopping malls. It plays during sporting events, religious services, and family holidays. After all, what would a birthday be without a "Happy Birthday" song?

Music makes us think and feel because it is a powerful source of energy and each day you have the opportunity to make the energy of music work for you. When you are down you can play a song that lifts your spirit and adds a kick to your step. When you are going to an important meeting or event, you can play a song that gives you confidence. When you are stressed and nervous you can play music that relaxes you. Music is energy that you can use to fuel your life whenever and wherever you need it.

 ACTION STEPS

1. Today's technology makes it very easy to energize your life with music. Most music stores now have machines that allow you to make custom CDs. Or you can use a computer to store your favorite CDs and with your computer and a CD burner you can make your own energizing CD.

2. Make a list of the songs that lift you up and create your custom CD or tape.

3. When you feel down or need a pick-me-up, find your song and play the music.

CONNECT WITH NATURE

All beings are encompassed within one all-encompassing great energy:
So I understood from the coolness of this morning's passing breeze.

MUMON

Ever wonder why people love the beach, the mountains and places like Central Park in New York City? Because they are powerful sources of energy. Whether it's the ocean air, the crashing waves, large trees or fields of green, when we visit these places we feel the positive energy of nature and it has a profound effect on our mind and body.

My friend Deb says that she gets her energy from the beach. She once told me, "The sunlight reflecting off the water gives me energy and the waves crashing on shore give me strength."

I have a friend, Brian, who loves to hike in the mountains. He says that he goes to the mountains to put his life in perspective. And many of the residents of New York City will tell you Central Park is where they recharge their batteries.

If you are like most people, you probably are reading this thinking, "Yes, I love these places. I feel great when I go there." And like most people it's probably been so long since you have tapped the energy of nature that you forgot how much you loved going to these places until you read this. Well, I urge you now to remember the feeling you get when you sit in the park, or feel hot sand on your feet, or stand under 100-year-old trees and let this feeling motivate you to take the time to connect with nature and enjoy the energy it will generously share with you.

ACTION STEPS

1. Visit a place of nature at least once a week. Pick a time and a day and make it a ritual. Take your lunch break in a nearby park.

2. Ride your bike to the beach. Take your kids hiking in the mountains. Go fishing at a nearby lake. Exercise with a friend in a park.

3. If you love golf, consider a visit to the golf course as beneficial as a trip to the park so long as you take the time to enjoy the air, the trees and the green grass.

4. Connect with nature and connect often.

KNOW WHAT
YOU ARE MADE OF

To see the world in a grain of sand. And heaven in a wild flower
To hold infinity in the palm of your hand. And eternity in an hour.

WILLIAM BLAKE

When we rub our hands together, they produce heat because we are energy. When we touch a person's hand we sometimes get shocked because we are energy. We often think we are a physical machine but in reality we are an energy machine consisting of approximately 75 trillion energy vibrating cells (I'm not sure who's counting but this is the approximate number of cells in the human body) that form one whole energy being. We often think that we are a physical machine because of our physical form but what we need to realize is that our energetic body is simply vibrating at a slow enough pace to appear solid. Just as water can take the form of steam or ice, our energy bodies on the outside appear solid whereas on the inside we are a river of change, ever flowing, ever changing.

Deepak Chopra, M.D., mind/body expert and author of *Quantum Healing and Perfect Health,* explains:

"Ninety-eight percent of the atoms in our bodies were not there a year ago. The carbon dioxide, oxygen and nitrogen is completely different from a year ago. The skeleton that seems so solid was not there three months ago. The framework is there but the atoms that make up the framework are constantly changing. Your skin is new every month. You have a new stomach lining every four days. It is as if you lived in a building whose bricks were systematically taken out and replaced every year."

Scientists know that we are a collection of electrons, protons, atoms and cells that vibrate at a slow enough speed to appear solid and form one large, energy being. However, you don't have to be a scientist to know that energy is all around us and inside us. Human beings, trees, water, sunlight, air, plants and every other single thing in the universe—they're all made of energy. Everything in life involves energy and energy has everything to do with you. Just because you can't see energy doesn't mean it doesn't exist. You can't see the energy transmission from a cell phone to the towers but we know it exists. We can call someone right now. When you're watching television via your dish you can't see the signals but they do exist.

Now you might be saying, "OK. I'm made of energy. What does that mean?" I will share with you now what I share with the people who attend my seminars. It means everything. Once you understand you are energy you begin to think, "If I am made of energy, then how can I fuel my life with the best sources of energy?" You understand the fact that if you want to live optimally you need optimum fuel. You realize without energy we couldn't survive and without quality energy an Energy Addict couldn't thrive. Dirty fuel results in a dirty motor while high octane fuel results in an energized mind, body and spirit.

 ACTION STEPS

1. As your read further you will find more positive energy to fuel your life. Simply tap into it whenever you need it.

PUT YOUR ENERGY FIRST

Imagine you're an energy vending machine. Your family comes up to you, puts a few coins in and says we need some energy. Do you have any to give or are you already spent? Are you stocked up or sold out? Or think about your boss standing by your machine. Now that's a scary thought. He is looking at you deciding if he wants a large or a small amount of energy today. Do you have the energy to give? There are a lot of people looking to put coins in us and if we don't have the energy to give, they'll likely bang on the machine looking for their money back. Let's just hope they don't tip the machine over. The fact is, we can't give what we don't have. To give energy we need to have energy. To have energy we need to put our energy first. This means that we need to stock up our vending machine before we give it to everyone else. While some may call this selfish, I call it smart. While some may call you self-centered I call you generous. If you put your energy first you will have more energy for yourself and more to share with others.

Consider Ted. Ted is always giving to everyone. He ignores his own needs, works tirelessly, gets little sleep and spends his free time making sure everyone else is happy. Everyone else receives his Energy but Ted has nothing left for himself. Everyone says, "WOW, look at how giving Ted is. Isn't he great?" But Ted's machine becomes empty. In the future Ted may burn out. Or Ted will likely get sick and will not be there for his family when they need him. Or Ted might leave his family to find so-called "happiness".

Now consider Ed. Ed puts his energy first. Ed stocks up on energy. Ed makes time for exercise, sleep, play and himself.

Ed takes care of himself so he has something left to give his family. Ed takes care of himself so he has more energy for his career. Ed knows that he can't give his energy if he doesn't have any for himself. In the end everyone in Ed's life is better off because Ed put his energy first.

So remember, even when society criticizes you for putting your energy first, be like Ed. This doesn't mean you are selfish. You put your energy first and then you share your energy with others. You get a massage so you will be more relaxed during the week. If you are a mom with small children, you hire that sitter for a few hours so you can recharge and rejuvenate. You take your lunch break in the park so you can be more productive in the afternoon. You exercise in the morning so you can spend time with your kids in the evening. You ask your husband or wife to watch the kids so you can take some time for yourself. You balance your personal life and career. In the long run everyone you live with, work with and interact with will thank you. Those who have the energy are the ones who can share it. Instead of handing out your energy to everyone else remember to first stock up your energy vending machine and then you can dispense your energy accordingly. When those who need you most put their quarters in, you'll have plenty of energy to give.

ACTION STEPS

1. Write down how you put everything and everyone else before your energy.

2. This week, write down one action you will take to put your energy first.

3. Take one action that puts your energy first. Do it again and again.

CREATE RITUALS THAT WILL BECOME YOUR FOUNDATION

The most accomplished performers have defined specific rituals in daily life where as those who are less successful do not.

JAMES E. LOEHR, ED.D, AUTHOR AND PSYCHOLOGIST

As part of any "energy for life" plan, rituals are the key to turning our goals into reality—or chaos into concrete. Rituals help us create positive habits that will become our foundation in a crazy world.

For example, when I was at the peak of my unhappiness several years ago I asked myself what was missing in my life. The answers were loud and clear—a healthy diet, exercise, creative expression, and time with my wife and kids. So I developed my routine and rituals around those very things. My wife and I decided to make Saturday night our date night; every Saturday we would hire a babysitter and go out for dinner and a movie. I started writing every night after I read to my daughter and put her down to sleep. It became a priority to get home each night so that I could spend time with her before she went to bed.

On the exercise and diet front I created exercise routines and diets and made them a part of my everyday life. I went to the same deli every morning and ordered four egg whites and fruit for breakfast before heading into work. I liked walking in the door and holding four fingers in the air; the cooks knew what to make. Amazingly, these routines and rituals helped bring a certain order and peace to my life that made everything flow much easier. My habits became my life and I was much happier.

By incorporating meaningful habits into our lives with rituals and routines, we make our lives more meaningful. This gives us a foundation and a center that we can build on and around. We can develop a routine or ritual for anything. Perhaps we walk our dog every night before we go to bed. Or we do yoga before we shower in the morning. We eat French toast every Sunday. We call our special friends once a month at the same time. If we are single, we might go to a social event once a week every Thursday. If we are married, we might call our spouse every day at noon to ask how he or she is doing. If we are religious, we most likely go to a religious service once a week. If we are spiritual, we likely meditate and pray daily.

Our life is the result of our words, choices, thoughts and actions. What we believe, say, choose and do is what we become. When you create rituals that increase your mental, physical and spiritual energy, you become more energetic, happier and successful.

 ACTION STEPS

1. As you read more of this book, write down the strategies that you want to incorporate into your life and decide what ritual will help you make it a habit. Use my action steps at the end of each section as a guide and decide the best times and days to incorporate each power source in your life.

2. Use my ritual planner below as a guide. You can easily re-create this ritual planner on a separate sheet of paper.

STRATEGY — Eat a healthy breakfast before work

ACTION — Eat breakfast

TIME — 7am

DAYS — Monday-Friday

3. Complete the ritual contract below and tape this to your mirror and carry a copy in your car. Also add this ritual schedule to your daily planner or calendar.

I will incorporate _____ into my life
                            strategy

by _____
              doing what

at _____on _____
       time   day(s)

Your contract might look something like:

I will incorporate a healthy breakfast into my life by eating breakfast at 7am, Monday thru Friday.

Signature_____

EXERCISE IN THE MORNING

A journey of a thousand miles begins with a single step.

CONFUCIUS

While everyone knows that exercise is good for them many people don't do it on a regular basis. "I don't have the time" is a common reason for not exercising. Or I often hear, "I'm too tired at the end of the day." Well, we now have increasing evidence that we don't need to exercise a long time to increase our energy. According to performance expert and researcher Martin Moore-Ede, M.D., Ph.D., "Even as little as a minute or so of light physical activity sends an immediate and powerful signal to your brain to reduce tension and increase alertness and energy."

And when people ask me the best time to exercise, I tell them that while anytime you are exercising is a good time, I recommend the morning as the best. When you exercise in the morning your body and brain work together to kick start your metabolism. Your brain tells your body, "Hey, we are going to be busy today, start producing some energy." Your body kicks in and starts burning fuel to provide the energy your brain says it needs. This helps increase your energy production and alertness.

Another benefit of morning exercise is that it is easier to make exercise a habit when we do it in the morning. If we wait until lunch or the end of the day it is more likely we will feel too tired to exercise and other obstacles will get in the way. According to Robert Cooper, Ph.D, a study by the Southwestern Health institute in Phoenix found that three out of four people who did some light morning exercise continued the exercise habit one year later. In comparison only half of those who waited until midday to exercise were able to keep up the habit and among those who said, "I'll do it in the evening," only one out of every four were still exercising a year after the study began.

 ACTION STEPS

1. Plan your exercise the night before. Lay out your exercise clothes on your dresser. This will help remind you of your commitment.

2. Do one form of light exercise. You can take a walk around your neighborhood. Walk up and down your stairs. Play and follow a Yoga video. Do pushups or abdominal stretches. If you have a stationary bike read the paper or a book while you pedal. Watch television while you walk on a treadmill. These are just a few ideas.

3. Remember, you don't need a gym or expensive equipment. All you need is a pair of shoes and place to walk.

4. Visit www.jorgecruise.com for simple exercises that only take eight minutes in the morning. And read Jorge's book *8 Minutes in the Morning*. It makes a lot of common sense.

DRINK WATER TO SURVIVE AND THRIVE

One of the simplest and most powerful things you can do to energize your life is to drink water. You are constantly losing water throughout the day and night through breathing, perspiration, urination and bowel movements. Studies show that a decrease in water consumption leads to fatigue and headaches. Vernon H. Mark, M.D., a neurosurgeon and co-author of *Brain Power* states, "Because a deficiency of water can alter the concentration of electrolytes such as sodium, potassium, and chloride, water has a profound effect on brain function and energy level." This makes sense since your body is made of mostly water and your body and brain work best when they are fully hydrated. Water helps deliver important nutrients, energy and messages to the various cells in your body. Water is the fuel your body and brain need to survive and thrive. Just as oil helps a car engine function optimally, water helps you operate at peak performance. And the best thing about water is you can find it everywhere.

ACTION STEPS

1. Most experts agree that the average person needs to drink six to eight cups of water every day to stay healthy. If you exercise you will likely need even more. So drink plenty of water.

2. Try to consume small amounts of water every 30 minutes during the day. This will keep you energized and

alert all day long. With each sip of water your brain tells your body, "Get ready, I have just filled you up with fuel for your life."

3. While water is better than soda, there are also brands of water that are better than others. Check out Penta Water at www.Pentawater.com . If water was gas, Penta Water would be considered high octane fuel.

NEUTRALIZE THE
ENERGY VAMPIRES

I will not let anyone walk through my mind with their dirty feet.

MAHATMA GANDHI

They lurk in our businesses, our families and our social organizations. They are real. They are everywhere. And they will suck the life out of you if you let them. If you're like most people, it has happened to you. You were talking to someone and before you knew it, they drained the life right out of you. You looked for fang marks on your neck but they were nowhere to be found. Then you realized Energy Vampires don't have fangs. They have other means to suck your energy.

Here are a few:

Negative comments—"Did I tell you how much I hate my life and work? Did I tell you what so and so did to me? Did I tell you how my life stinks? Did I tell you why nothing goes right?"

Dream snatching—"You can't do that. How are you going to do that? Are you living in fantasyland? Get back to the real world. You should do this instead."

Shrinking devices—"What is wrong with you? Can you do anything right? You are the worst. I hate working with you."

In other situations the words may be less harsh but the result ends up being the same. Once an Energy Vampire starts sucking it is difficult to break free. Don't let this happen. Instead be prepared to neutralize an Energy Vampire from the beginning. You don't need a stake or garlic. Here are four techniques:

 **ACTION STEPS**

1. Look in the mirror. Sometimes we are the Vampires. If we pay attention to our thoughts and words we can eliminate the Vampire in us. Are you being negative or positive? I ask myself this often. If you are being negative stop the following things:

≈ Stop judging.
≈ Stop gossiping.
≈ Stop saying negative things.

2. Confront and reform. Tell your Energy Vampire (EV) that he or she is being negative. They may not even realize it. Ask for support, positive feedback and encouragement from them. If your EV is a colleague, family member or friend, perhaps you can reform them into an Energy Addict. Show them how to spread positive energy. If they just don't see it or refuse to do it then you may have to give an ultimatum. You might say, "This is my goal. This is where I am going and if you're going to be negative then I can't be around you."

3. Turn on the Light. When you were a child and scared of the dark you turned on the light and felt better. Negative energy is like darkness. When you encounter an Energy Vampire, turn on the light. When an EV comes at you with fear, negativity, hate and anger turn on the light and respond with love, kindness, and positive energy. Negative energy is powerless in the light. Think about what happens when someone gets mad and yells at you. If you don't yell back, they lose momentum and power. If you return with kindness they lose even

more power. On the other hand, if you yell back then the negative energy grows and grows.

4. Run. Run as far and as fast as you can. This sometimes is the best technique if you are not close with the EV. You only have so much energy and in today's world you need to keep all you have. If, for example, you are in the grocery store and you see someone who drains your energy then run away fast. Really fast.

5. Identify one EV in your life and decide what technique you will use to neutralize them.

ADD THE ENERGY
OF PLAY TO YOUR DAY

*If you wish to glimpse inside a human soul, just watch a person laugh and play.
Those who laugh and play well are the most alive.*

FYODOR DOSTOYEVSKY

Did you know that children laugh about 400 times a day while adults laugh only about 25 times? If you need more energy for your life and career then add a little play to your day. When you play your life flows easier and your day flows faster. If you have forgotten how to play simply watch children. They will show you the way. Children always seem to have boundless energy and perhaps it is because they are always laughing and playing. They are full of life, energy and smiles. Without a thought for tomorrow they truly enjoy the present. With two children, ages five and three, having fun and not being stressed has been one of the big challenges in my life. While they played I would worry about them getting hurt or dirty. I often wished that someone would write "Don't Sweat the Little People." But through this challenge I have learned that if I behave more like them and less like a stressed-out adult, I will be happier and so will my family. When it comes to play, my children are my teachers.

Here are a few ways to add the energy of play to your day.

ACTION STEPS

1. Tell a joke. Make someone laugh today and you'll find yourself laughing as well. In California, the new rage is laughing clubs where people get together and simply laugh.

2. Smile. The simple act of smiling can improve your mood and increase your energy.

3. Play with your kids. Roll around the grass with them. Play tag. Eat ice cream together.

4. Dance the night away. Sometimes when I'm writing during the day or night, my wife will put on music downstairs. I'll walk down from my office and she and the kids will be jumping around and dancing. At first they look funny because I'm in writing mode but once I get into dancing with them I feel energized and rejuvenated. Plus the visual of my little kids dancing just makes me laugh.

5. Get back to your favorite hobby. Remember that thing that you loved doing. Make time once a day or at least once a week to do it.

6. Play at work. My friend Teddy works on Wall Street. Teddy is famous for having fun and playing games. Even at work Teddy finds a way to play. He tries to answer the phone quicker than anyone in his company. While this may be silly to some, for Teddy it makes him sharper and his day flow faster. What can you do to make work more fun?

7. Play after work. My friend Amy is a pharmaceutical rep by day and comedian by night. Doing what she loves after work makes her more fulfilled and productive during the day.

BREATHE IN ENERGY AND BREATHE OUT TODAY'S WORRIES

One of the most simple and powerful ways to increase your energy is to breathe. That's right. Breathe. We all do it but sometimes we forget to do it right. When you get stressed, research tells us, you take shorter breaths and less oxygen into your lungs. This means less oxygen in your brain and body and less energy for you. So as you live, work, shop, clean, run errands - did I say work - do the laundry, get together with friends, make time for family and attack your to-do list, remember simply to breathe. Monitor yourself and ask "Am I stressed? Am I breathing?" Each time you feel yourself getting stressed, focus on your breathing. Take in five to 10 deep breaths. Breathe in energy and breathe out today's worries.

ACTION STEPS

Practice your energizer breath now.

1. Get comfortable. Loosen your shoulders and neck.

2. Exhale completely.

3. Inhale through your nose for a silent count of three.

4. Hold your breath for a few seconds.

5. Exhale through your mouth for a silent count of four (focus on your breathing).

6. Repeat five to 10 times (imagine each breath fueling you up with breathing).

7. Repeat steps 1-6 when necessary.

FOCUS YOUR ENERGY

Most people have no idea of the giant capacity we can immediately command when we focus all of our resources on mastering a single area of our lives.

ANTHONY ROBBINS

What turns an idea into a reality? A vision into a painting? Words into a poem? Like everything in nature we possess the enormous power to focus energy in order to create. The miraculous power of a woman's body to channel and focus the necessary energy to create and birth a baby is one of nature's greatest gifts. While not everyone has the ability to create human life we all have the power to give life to our ideas, plans, and dreams. We can birth a painting, a building, an invention. Everything we create is a result of our focused energy. In one state, energy is passive—sitting and waiting to be used. A pen sitting on a table. A plan not yet read. A road not yet taken. In another state, energy is scattered—a fire out of control, a person being pulled in a thousand different directions. In the desired state, energy is focused. The words written, a plan acted upon, a person in pursuit of his or her goals.

Consider two different projects. At one project site we see a completed building 30 stories high. At the other project site we see tools sitting on a floor, unmixed concrete, and workers playing catch with a baseball. The only difference between the two projects is energy that has been channeled, focused and applied rather than scattered and wasted. Energy is everywhere and we all have an opportunity to use it. We can either let it sit there or make it work for us.

We have the opportunity every day to channel our scattered energy into focused energy. We can grab the energy being scattered and wasted on things we don't really want and focus that energy on creating the life we do want. Just as an architect designs a building, we have the ability to design our life. The design determines what we build, the tools and materials needed and the energy required.

We must first decide what we want to create. What will our life's design be like? Then we must concentrate on building our life. Just as a builder applies his or her energy to transform the design into reality, we must grab a set of tools, focus our actions, thoughts and words and create our life—one positive thought—one action at a time.

Here are a few tools to help you focus your energy.

 ACTION STEPS

1. Write down what you want to create. These are your goals. The act of writing your goals begins the process of transforming your thoughts into your reality. For instance, one of your goals might be to increase your energy.

2. Decide what steps are necessary to achieve your goals. Where and how must you invest and focus your energy in order to make your goals come to life? Then write them down. List them. One, two, three. If your goal is to increase your energy you might write:

≈ Eat breakfast.
≈ Exercise in the morning.
≈ Have more fun.

3. Create a schedule and/or plan to incorporate your action steps into your life. Only create a schedule that you can commit to. For this example you might write:

• Eat breakfast before work Monday-Friday. Eat breakfast by 7am.

• Do 5-10 minutes of exercise Monday-Thursday at 6:30am.

• Play a game with the kids after dinner Monday and Wednesday.

4. Add this schedule to your calendar or planner. It needs to be as important as a meeting with your doctor.

5. Think about any roadblocks that can get in the way of you, your energy and your goals. Write down these roadblocks and decide how you will laser through them if they appear. Knowing how you are going to deal with your roadblocks now will make you successful later. For example, a roadblock for eating breakfast might be having to rush out the door because you wake up too late. The solution is to not hit the snooze button and give yourself time to eat an energizing breakfast. Another solution is to go to bed earlier and wake more rested.

6. Now focus and take action. Follow your plan. Focus your energy. Create your life.

7. Monitor your progress. Track your results. Enjoy your accomplishments. Remember, if you focus you will create.

ZOOM FOCUS ON
THE LITTLE THINGS

In addition to focusing your energy to achieve your goals there is another kind of focus you will need. While focusing on your yearly and weekly goals represent a big picture focus there is something I call Zoom Focus. Zoom Focus is all about focusing day-to-day and minute-to-minute.

In today's hurried technology driven society Zoom Focus is more important than ever. One of my core philosophies is that success is all about the little things and each day the difference between success and failure is—the little things. Little phone calls can waste precious time. Little disruptions can disturb critical moments of concentration. And little interruptions that come in many forms can waste your most valuable asset—your energy. Zoom Focus means we focus on doing the right little things that lead to success and stop letting the wrong little things from wasting our time and energy.

As someone who has owned high-energy restaurants, I have trained my managers on focusing on the little things and they can attest they have been the difference between our success and failure. What I shared with them, I would like to share with you now in the following action steps. I believe using Zoom Focus techniques will make you more focused, energetic and successful and less scattered.

ACTION STEPS

1. Carry a small notebook or planner with you.

2. In the morning before you go to work or right when

you get to work write down your priorities for the today. What are the little things you need to focus on today? Today it may be paperwork.

3. Then write down the little road blocks that can get in the way. What has become a road block in the past and what do you anticipate blocking your focus today. For example if you planned on getting a lot of paper work done today one of the road blocks might be phone calls and emails from friends and family.

4. Decide how you will laser through your little road blocks. Create your strategy ahead of time. In this case you might decide to not look at your email and not answer your phone or check messages until you are done with paper work.

5. Repeat daily and watch how Zoom Focus turns little successes into big results.

BE YOUR OWN BOSS

No bird soars too high if he soars with his own wings.

WILLIAM BLAKE

The most important thing you can do when creating your life is to be your own boss. Everything else feeds off of this one thing. You can't create if you are not in charge of your creation. So repeat after me. You will become your own boss! You will become your own boss!

Sure, you most likely have a boss at work. We all have to report to someone at sometime in our professional life. Even CEOs report to a group of bosses called a board of directors. However, when you become your own boss you are saying to yourself and to the world that you are responsible and in charge of your own energy and your life. Your work boss controls and manages your workflow, work schedule, and other work activities such as travel, meetings, and conferences. On the other hand, you and only you are in charge of your energy, your life flow, your life schedule and your lifestyle. You may have to be on a plane for a meeting in California, but it's up to you to decide how you spend your time and what you eat on the plane. Your boss may give you a certain amount of time to finish the latest project; yet, it is up to you to incorporate that project into your routine and not let it take over your life.

Remember, this is your life and you will no longer let the traveling, the projects, and the work take over your life. You will no longer sit on the plane, at your desk or on your couch and let everything else control you. Being your own boss means being an Energy Addict. You are a conscious, thinking, energized being who is the creator of your life. Any situation, any event, any problem, is taken in, digested, addressed and mastered. You realize that you and only you are accountable for your life. You stop blaming others for any and every problem in your life and you start making yourself happy and successful.

Note that it's not easy to be your own boss. Many of us would rather people tell us what to do instead of deciding for ourselves. We might not want the responsibility of being in charge of our own life. Or maybe we are not up for the challenge. We don't always want to make the tough decisions and resist temptations. We would rather be created than be a creator. However, once you become your own boss and feel better than you ever have in your life, you will never be able to imagine living any other way. You'll realize by investing a little more energy to be your own boss you will actually have more energy in return. And you'll have even more energy because you won't waste any more time or energy blaming others. Once you see yourself as both a creator and a creation of your own focused energy, intention and actions, you will seek and grasp brief moments of time that allow you to create true success.

 ACTION STEPS

1. Write down one area of your life where you can take more responsibility for your own actions. For example you might write, "During my lunch break I can make decisions that will benefit me."

2. Next write down several actions you can take that will benefit you during this time. For example you might write, "I will eat a healthier lunch. I will get fresh air during my lunch break. I will take deep breaths and prepare positively for the day ahead."

3. Repeat steps for each area of your life where you would like to be more in control.

MAKE A DIFFERENCE

If you find it in your heart to care for somebody else, you will have succeeded.

MAYA ANGELOU

There is a simple law of the universe called Karma that says, "what you give, you will receive" and "if you do good things for others, good things will happen to you." My Grandmother used to say the same thing in one of her favorite phrases, "What comes around goes around." I believe that it is impossible to truly thrive in life unless we put forth the energy to make a difference in other people's lives. No matter how busy we are and no matter how many things we have going on in life, we need to find the time to make a difference. Not just because good things will happen to us, but also because it is a natural part of the laws of energy and life that make the world work. Just as we take in energy through food and expend energy through exercise, we also receive energy from others and give energy to the world. We give. We receive. We help. We get helped. We give of ourselves to others and positive things happen to us.

There are many ways we can make a difference in people's lives. The first thing that might come to mind is volunteering. Many people during the holidays volunteer at homeless shelters for Thanksgiving and Christmas. We can also volunteer on a regular basis at a women's shelter, at a Boys and Girls Club or a YMCA. We can become a big sister or brother, a member of the Rotary, Lions, or Kiwanis clubs, a mentor to a high school student interested in business, a coach of a youth athletic team, a music teacher, a computer teacher, a guest speaker at local middle school, a Sunday School teacher at church or choose from a thousand other volunteer projects that are available in our local communities. Many organizations such as The United Way have weekend volunteer projects and choices for professionals who have no time during the week. The opportunities are out there. It's up to you to choose what feels right to you.

We can also make a difference with our hearts and our wallets, as well. We can financially give to charities and causes that are dear to us. My wife lost both of her parents to cancer, so she is very supportive of cancer research. We can support a local school program. Buy Girl Scout cookies. Give to our religious and/or spiritual organizations. Buy a computer for a school or youth organization. The choices are endless and so is the need. When we give we help to fill a void in someone's life and we fill a void in ours as well.

We can also make a difference by organizing and planning fundraisers and creating awareness of specific causes and problems. It takes a tremendous amount of time and energy to mobilize people around a cause and an event. There are also a lot of problems in society that are not brought to our attention and it is important that people are educated and informed so they can do something to help. Those who take on this role are not only filling a great need; they are generating an impact that is felt long after the event or awareness campaign is over.

While living in Atlanta, I started a non-profit organization called the Phoenix Organization. We united thousands of Atlanta's young professionals to raise money and volunteer for youth focused charities. Through this experience I discovered that it is amazing what we can accomplish when a lot of people give just a little time and a big piece of their heart.

ACTION STEPS

1. Decide what charities, programs, or schools are meaningful to you. What motivates you to take action? Children,

elderly, homeless, education, etc?

2. Decide how you would like to get involved. Would you like to fundraise, plan events, volunteer with people, deliver food, etc.

3. Determine when you are available. After work, during the day, during lunch?

4. Make a commitment to yourself. Use the tool below to help you keep your commitment.

I_____ commit to helping
        name

_____
        organization

by_____
        doing what

on_____
        what day(s)

at_____
        time available

BE CONTAGIOUS

The world is like a mirror, you see? Smile and your friends smile back.

JAPANESE ZEN SAYING

Positive Energy Addiction is one addiction we want to be contagious. In sports, winning is contagious. Losing is contagious. And positive energy is contagious.

Confidence can spread throughout an entire baseball team and lead to a surge of hits and home runs. In contrast, one batter's slump and hitless streak can affect the entire lineup.

Life is no different. Each day we have hundreds of interactions that affect millions of people. To understand this fact, let's take a helicopter ride to about 500 feet in the air. We look down and what do we see? People scurrying about—running, walking, and driving next to each other. They get on buses next to strangers and chat. They talk to people in the grocery store. They go to restaurants, movies and malls to be around other people. Go up another 1,000 feet and we see they live in neighborhoods, towns and cities where they share the same water, and breathe the same air. Now, let's take the helicopter even higher. We see them take roads connecting communities, cities and states. As we go higher, we see that even states and countries and continents are connected by planes, boats, telephones and now the internet. The higher we go, the more we realize just how interconnected we all are. Human beings always find ways to connect, whether it's a bridge, a boat, or over the internet.

Because we are connected to so many people, each day we have the opportunity to be contagious and share positive energy with those near to us and those far away. A pat on the back to a co-worker can make all the difference. A compliment to a friend can change their entire day. A smile and a kind word to a grocery clerk can have ripple effects beyond your imagination. Who knows how many people the grocery clerk made laugh and smile because of you? And who knows how many of those people went home and were nicer to their children? When I e-mail my newsletter to thousands of people I often wonder who it has been forwarded to and how it has impacted their lives. I don't even know them and yet my positive energy has been shared with them. In writing this book I hope to share positive energy with you in the hope you will share it with others. Together we can be contagious and spread positive energy to our co-workers, family, friends and strangers. And so on and so on.

 ACTION STEPS

1. Be contagious.

2. Remember to smile and smile often.

3. Give hugs (when appropriate), pats on the back, handshakes and high fives, BILLY!

4. Compliment people often.

5. Make others feel good about themselves while being sincere.

6. Share good news, great stores and happy endings with your co-workers and/or family.

7. Become an Energy Addict Sponsor. (page 225)

FEED YOUR BODY LIFE

Today more than ever, we need to fuel our bodies with the best sources of energy. We need to eat real foods that fuel our passion, our drive, and our busy schedule. We need to feed our body life. To do this I recommend that people eat whole foods or in other words, foods from nature. Whole foods are foods that have not been processed. They come from nature and they have a short shelf life and usually contain one or two ingredients. Several examples include raisins, nuts, apples, beans, rice, spinach, salmon, eggs, lean meats and bananas. This differs from processed foods that can sit on a shelf a long time, contain 5 or more ingredients made up of three to five syllable words we can't pronounce and often contain partially hydrogenated oils and preservatives to give them a longer shelf life. Look on any super market shelf and you'll find mostly processed foods. The simple fact is that our natural bodies perform best when fed natural foods. Just as a car engine needs high quality fuel to run properly we need high quality energy to ensure peak performance. Foods from nature contain the most and best sources of energy where as most processed foods are made up of empty calories with little energy or benefit to us. While it is difficult to make whole foods 100% of your diet simply do your best to incorporate more fresh fruit, vegetables, legumes, whole grains and lean meats into your diet. While there is much confusing and conflicting information and research regarding the best diets to lose weight, the research is clear that if we eat more fresh vegetables, fruits, whole grains and learn sources of protein we increase our chances that we will live longer, healthier, more energetic lives. No matter what diet you may be on in the short run, remember that in the long run our bodies do best when fed nature's energy. To help you incorporate high energy sources of fuel into your life try the following simple action steps. You will feel the difference.

 ACTION STEPS

1. Think of food as fuel. Eat foods closest to nature so you build your body everyday with the best sources of energy.

2. When choosing your foods read the labels on everything you buy so you know what you are putting into your body. For example, Smuckers all natural peanut butter is made with just peanuts and salt. Wow. What a concept. Peanut butter made with just peanuts and a little salt. Where many other brands, also sold in supermarkets, are full of sugar, hydrogenated oils and chemicals.

3. Reduce the amount of processed foods in your diet.

4. Eat almonds, pumpkin seeds and walnuts. I try to eat a handful a day. They are a great source of energy and healthy fat. While many people say "I can't eat nuts, they're fattening." I tell them only if you eat the entire jar or bag. Research tells us we need to eat good sources of fat to burn fat. Grab a handful and put the rest away.

5. Incorporate flaxseeds into your diet. They are great sources of omega- 3 essential fatty acids which are healthy fats. Sprinkle ground flax seeds on your cereal or oatmeal or use flax oil instead. You can buy flax seeds and oil in your local health food store or Whole Foods Market.

6. Simply add fruit with your breakfast and vegetables with lunch and dinner for more live foods in your diet. Buy your fruit and vegetables on Sunday and have them ready for

the week. For example, my wife will often add three carrot sticks on our children's lunch or dinner plate. A simple addition adds vitamins and nutrients to their bodies.

7. Instead of chips and candy bars, eat a handful of nuts and raisins as a snack.

8. Eat a piece of fruit and yogurt in the afternoon between lunch and dinner.

9. If you eat meat, which many of us do, look for hormone free and antibiotic free meat. They are the most natural. Whole Foods Market carries only hormone free and antibiotic free meets. Many grocery stores are also starting to carry them as well. Ask your store for more information.

10. Eat more salmon. Salmon is a great source of Omega-3's.

11. Eat eggs in moderation. The medical community now says that three to four eggs a week is Ok. They are concerned with cholesterol in the egg yolks. I will keep an eye on this because this may change in the future as there is debate of whether or not cholesterol in food actually increases cholesterol in the body. Until the research is clear, I will continue to eat four or five whole eggs per week and a lot of egg whites. Eggs are a great source of B-vitamins, minerals, protein and iron. I love to start my morning with eggs and fruit.

12. Drink water instead of soda.

13. Remember, small simple changes make all the difference.

DON'T BUY THE BULL

Too often I see people pumping Mountain Dew, coffee, soda and energy drinks into their mouths as they look for a quick buzz and a jolt of energy to help them work harder and faster. When the caffeine high wears off they guzzle another one or grab a candy bar for a sugar high. Others drink coffee after coffee.

Yes, in the short run this may work. The caffeine and sugar may give you a quick boost of energy. But like any drug, they wear off and to keep the high going you need more and more and more. The problem is that when you rely on caffeine and sugar for energy instead of healthy foods you are setting yourself up for fatigue and burnout.

According to Dr. Andrew Weil, author of *8 Weeks to Optimum Health,* sugar has strong drug-like effects in some people. Sugar can give you a rush of energy, followed by a metabolic crash soon after. He says, "This cycle is extremely disruptive to the body's energy cycle and can trigger disturbing mood swings." And caffeine may stimulate stress hormones that give you temporary energy but also affect your natural energy cycle. Excessive caffeine and sugar give you the appearance they are supplying you with energy but in reality they drain the life out of you. The old adage "what goes up, must come down," often rings true. And while caffeine and sugar may take your energy sky high they also cause it to come crashing down.

To stop the crashing you have to keep filling your body with these energy sources and so begins the process I call a vicious cycle. I see it all the time as I travel around the country. Instead of eating food, drinking water and getting enough sleep people try to stay energized with caffeine. People wonder why they don't have any energy. They wonder why they are always tired and I believe relying on caffeine instead of food, sleep and water for energy is one of the main reasons. They are living on short bursts, quick fixes and a bunch of bull instead of the real power sources that will provide them with fuel for life.

EAT BREAKFAST

Many of us think that if we want to lose weight then we should skip breakfast. After all, if we don't eat breakfast that means less calories. Right? Ironically one of the keys to losing weight, and increasing your metabolism is to eat a hearty and healthy breakfast. And one of the simplest things you can do to increase your energy during the day is to eat breakfast.

When you eat breakfast you activate your thermic switch which helps you burn fat and produce energy throughout the day. Studies show if you eat breakfast you are more alert and you perform better at work. Breakfast eaters also show less fatigue and are usually leaner than those who skip breakfast.

According to Dr. Sarah Leibiwitz, Ph.D., of the Rockefeller University in New York City, when you skip breakfast you are also more likely to gorge on high fat, high sugar foods at night. Many of us can attest to this in our own struggles with gaining and losing weight. If we skip meals throughout the day, when it is time to eat we often lose control. So instead of gulping a cup of coffee and running out the door, make time for a quick and healthy breakfast. Here are three action steps to help you make breakfast a regular part of your day.

ACTION STEPS

1. Plan. Decide what you are going to eat for breakfast the night before so when you wake up tired and sluggish you already have a clear plan of action.

2. Make it healthy. Pop-Tarts and high sugar cereals don't

count. You might as well eat a candy bar. Instead, eat foods high in fiber, high in protein and low in fat. Here are several examples of a great breakfast.

≈ Oatmeal with low fat milk and a piece of fruit.

≈ Three eggs, a piece of fruit and a slice of whole grain bread.

≈ A bowl of low fat plain yogurt mixed with low fat granola, a cut-up banana and raisins.

≈ Whole grain toast with Smuckers all natural peanut butter.

3. Make time for breakfast. Get up 10 minutes earlier. All it takes is a few more minutes in the morning. Think of it this way: a few minutes to eat breakfast will give you hours of increased energy and productivity. It's worth it.

EXPERIENCE NEWNESS

The goal in life is to die young—as late as possible.

ASHLEY MONTAGU, PH.D., PROFESSOR IN THE DEPARTMENT
OF ANTHROPOLOGY AT RUTGERS UNIVERSITY

My 85-year-old Grandpa Eddy still writes, plays the piano and travels the country by train to visit family and friends. To him everything is new once again. He told me once that each morning he gets the local paper and reads the events section. He goes down the list and says, "Yes," "Yes," "Yes." " Yes" to a new museum exhibit. "Yes" to a light parade. "Yes" to everything.

I remember a few years ago when I took Grandpa Eddy to the Atlanta Botanical Garden. I watched as he savored the sight and smell of hundreds of flowers and plants with child like curiosity and awe. I understand now, what I felt then; that Grandpa Eddy understands when we are open to new things, new people, new places and new events we allow more energy into our lives. This energy stimulates our mind and body. It prevents rust from forming and keeps us sharp, alert, fun and young.

Experts and researchers agree the less we ask of our mind and body the less we will get in return. Human beings need new experiences in order to grow and evolve. If we are not growing, we are dying. It's a part of evolution. We need to engage our senses to stay young and energized. Think about a challenge in your life that helped you grow as a person. If you never experienced this challenge you would not be the person you are today.

Or think about what happens when you don't use the muscles in your body. They waste away. I still remember my broken arm as a young boy. When the doctors took the cast off, my arm was half its original size. On the contrary, when we lift weights we notice that our muscles grow in response to this new stimulus. In much the same way, every new experience, every new person we meet, every new event we attend helps us grow into fully energized, fully alive people.

William James said, "We must not just patch and tinker with life. We must keep renewing it." In this spirit let us continually renew our mind, body and spirit by fueling our lives with new experiences.

 ACTION STEPS

1. Say "Yes" to everything.

2. Get out of the house and meet new people.

3. Attend the new play or movie that just opened.

4. Go to a museum.

5. Try a new dinner recipe.

6. Take up a new hobby.

7. Buy a new CD.

8. Drive home a different way from work.

9. Learn a new word each day.

10. Take trips and visit new places.

CONNECT

The doors we open and close each day decide the lives we live.

FLORA WHITTEMORE

How many times has it happened to us? A friend introduces us to a friend of a friend and that leads to a job, a business deal or a date or even an entirely new life path. Who told you about your job? Who introduced you to the last decision maker that bought your product or signed a partnership with your company? If you applied for a new job, whom would you include in the reference section? How did you meet your significant other?

Many times, our world can get pretty hectic and the things that help us in life are the very things we stop doing. One of the first few things to go out the window during times of stress is our desire to reach out and meet new people or talk to those we already know. Yet, our relationships and our ability to meet and attract new people into our lives are our most valued treasures and attributes.

Everyone we meet is a potential friend, contact, business partner, co-worker, etc. When we are open to meeting new people the possibilities are endless and our world is limitless. The more people we connect with, the more energy we create for ourselves and others. Some like to use the term six degrees of separation that describes the simple truth that we are all connected by at most six people. This means that you and anyone in the world are only separated by six people. In today's world, which is getting smaller and smaller as communication and transportation becomes cheaper, easier and faster, I would say the reality is more like four degrees of separation.

Think about all of the almost improbable experiences that happen in your life. You're at the airport and you start talking to the person seated next to you and it turns out they know your old friend from high school. Or you are in another country and you meet someone who has a cousin that went to college with your brother. We talk to a stranger and find out they know an old friend of ours who they met through one of their friends.

You never know whom you are going to meet when you attend an association meeting or professional happy hour with hundreds of other people in your industry. The possibilities are endless when you accept a lunch invitation with a friend who has someone she wants you to meet or when you call an old friend and exchange updates. No matter how much work we have on our desk or how many items are still on our to-do list, we need to slow down enough to reach out and connect with new people and old friends. When we connect we energize ourselves and others.

 ACTION STEPS

1. Call an old friend you haven't spoken to in a while.

2. Accept a dinner invitation from your new neighbors.

3. Host a house party and invite people you want to get to know better.

4. Ask a co-worker to join you for lunch.

5. For new mothers like my wife, join a play group.

ENERGIZE YOUR STRENGTHS

Just do what you do best.

RED AUERBACH

According to Robert K. Cooper, Ph.D., author of *"The Other 90 Percent"*, it takes an enormous amount of time, effort and energy to raise an area of poor performance to mediocre performance. In contrast, it takes very little time and effort to raise an area of good performance to great performance as long as you're doing something that you enjoy.

Therefore, if we want to maximize our energy and apply it where it will make the biggest impact we should spend our time doing things we are good at and enjoy. While I may seem to be stating the obvious, how many of us spend our time trying to cover up or improve our weaknesses rather than cultivating our strengths? We spend most of our time and energy in the wrong profession or the wrong job doing daily tasks that don't match our skill sets or passion. This mismatch doesn't provide us with an outlet to develop our natural attributes nor does it allow us to realize our full potential. This causes us to waste time trying to become average rather than working to become great. The most successful people identify their strengths and weaknesses and focus their energies on energizing their strengths rather than wasting their time trying to improve their weaknesses.

Of course we're not going to make the most of our energy if we spend a lot of time doing things we don't love and are not naturally inclined to do. If we watch Venus Williams play tennis, Madonna sing, Robin Williams act, Michael Dell lead a company, or Rudy Guilianni run a city, we clearly see people who have cultivated certain talents that are as natural to them as breathing and eating. The result is that they excel. Like watching a seagull fly over the ocean, we can't take our eyes off them. It is no different for you and me. If we know our natural strengths and work to develop these attributes, we too will make the most of our energy and create amazing results.

 ACTION STEPS

1. List your skills. What do you do better than most people you know?

2. Write down what you love to do. What activities energize you? Identify what comes natural to you.

3. Write down one of your strengths and list several actions you will take to cultivate this strength.

4. Spend time each day and/or week to cultivate this strength.

BE THE AGE
YOU WANT TO BE

Youth has no age.

PABLO PICASSO

Baseball great Satchel Paige once asked, "How old would you be if you didn't know how old you are?" Satchel was over 40 the entire time he pitched in the major leagues, but no one really knew how old he was since his birth date always remained a mystery. In 1965, 59 years after Satchel's estimated birth year, he pitched for the last time, throwing three scoreless innings for the Kansas City Athletics. It is said that Satchel rarely answered questions about his age and when he did he would reply with something like, "Age is a question of mind over matter. If you don't mind, it doesn't matter."

Considering Satchel's philosophy about age, ask yourself how old you feel. Do you feel younger than your chronological age but always remind yourself that you are too old to be doing "this" and "that?" Or do you feel a lot older than you are and often say something like "I'm getting old. I'm not a kid anymore." I know many 60- and 70-year-olds who feel and act younger than people half their age. I also know some 40- and 50-year-olds who feel and look like they are 20 years older than their age. No matter what age you are now, as you get chronologically older you have the option to be the age you want to be. You can feel younger and grow younger at any age. Just forget how old you are and remember how young you want to be. It's all a matter of your mind. If you feel young and think young you will project youthful energy. When you are open to the possibility that anything is possible at any age, your body will be able to do things you never imagined.

Consider that former astronaut and Senator John Glenn went back in space at the age of 77 and former President George H.W. Bush sky dove from an air plane in his 70s. I work out at the gym with men and women in their 60s who are in better shape than me. My parents go out dancing more than people half their age. Examples of people being the age they want to be are everywhere. It seems Satchel Paige had the right idea. When we don't think about the age we are, we are free to be the age we want to be.

 ACTION STEPS

1. Decide right now the age you want to be.

2. Act and feel that you are that age.

3. Observe how your energy increases.

4. When people ask you how old you are respond with, "Age is a question of mind over matter. If you don't mind, it doesn't matter."

5. Read *Grow Younger, Live Longer* by Deepak Chopra, M.D. and David Simon, M.D.

DON'T BE TOO BUSY
FOR LUNCH

It's a popular notion that we will get more done if we skip lunch. I know, since I used to buy into this belief as well. Today hundreds of thousands of people, if not millions, will skip lunch in order to accomplish more at work. They'll say, "I have too much to do. I can't make lunch today." Or, "Lunch is a waste of time. I'll tough it out and get more done." "I'm swamped. No time for lunch." I know since these were a few of my sayings.

Unfortunately they couldn't be farther from the truth. Etienne Grandjean, M.D., Ph.D., an expert on productivity at the Swiss Federal Institute of Technology, says eating a good lunch is highly recommended "for both health and work efficiency." According to various studies, researchers agree that performance scores plunge when people skip lunch and those who skip lunch soon feel more anxious and tense. Skipping lunch can also slow your metabolism and cut your energy production throughout the day and lead to a ravenous appetite at dinner time. And Wayne Callaway M.D., clinical professor at George Washington University School of Medicine and Health Sciences, says, "People who skip breakfast or lunch tend to get more tired and binge in the evening, instead of eating moderately and having more energy throughout the day."

Ironically, the desire to get ahead and get more done actually leads to less productivity and burn-out if lunch is skipped on a regular basis. People will often try to compensate for their lack of energy by drinking coffee or caffeinated drinks instead of eating lunch. However, this simply makes a bad mistake worse by causing your body and brain to work harder and harder on less fuel. Our bodies need to recharge with a relaxing lunch break and a satisfying lunch and instead we're making our motors work beyond capacity. Eventually our motors will burn out.

Thankfully, the solution is simple. Whether you're a mom in the middle of running errands with her kids, a CEO in the middle of a major reorganization, or a college student studying for an exam, DON'T SKIP LUNCH. Ignore the temptation to skip lunch in order to get more done by remembering the facts that it doesn't work. Realize if you make time for lunch you will more than make up for this time with an increase in productivity and energy. Think of it this way. A 20-minute lunch will provide you with hours of energy. It's worth it.

EAT AN ENERGIZING LUNCH

So now you know that it's important to make time for lunch. Now the questions are, how do I make lunch a habit and what should I eat? While the answers can be an entire book in itself and many have been written, here are a few tips to help you make lunch an energizing part of your day.

1. Plan your meals the night before. Experts say that we make between 20 and 30 food choices a day. If we make these choices when we are so hungry we can't even think we are more likely to go through the fast-food drive thru than eating a healthy lunch. Planning your meals the night before sets you up for success. When planning decide whether you will eat outside or inside the office or home. Decide what restaurant you will visit and what you will order. If you decide to eat in the office or home it would be a great idea to prepare your lunch that night. That way when you get hungry, lunch is ready.

2. There's nothing worse than eating a huge lunch and then feeling horrible the rest of the day. The key is to eat a big enough lunch to satisfy you but not so big that you need a nap afterwards. I used to eat so much food at lunch that I felt useless the rest of the day. Now I eat lunches that don't put me to sleep and if I find myself getting filled up I ask for a to-go box and eat the rest as a mid-afternoon snack.

3. Remember to eat whole foods. No matter what diet you may be trying, the best source of fuel for our body and brain are foods from nature. Instead of white processed bread choose whole grain bread. Instead of fat-filled processed foods, choose

whole grains, beans, legumes, fruits, and vegetables.

4. Nutrition experts also recommend we include some protein as part of our lunch. Proteins such as turkey, chicken, fish, and lean meat take longer to digest which sustains our blood sugar level and keeps us from being hungry again soon after lunch.

5. Consider the case of the peanut butter and jelly sandwich when making choices for lunch. For the bread you can choose whole grain bread instead of white bread. For the peanut butter you can choose all natural peanut butter from brands such as Smuckers instead of the processed peanut butter laden with hydrogenated oils and sugar. For the jelly you can choose all natural fruit preserves such as Palmer All Fruit instead of fructose corn-sweetened, sugar-laden jelly. The little differences in these choices will make a big difference to your energy and health.

6. Other energizing lunch choices include:

≈ Salad with low fat dressing and grilled chicken or fish

≈ Southwest Burrito with chicken or tofu, lettuce, salsa, peppers and onions

≈ Turkey on whole grain bread with lettuce and tomato

≈ Sushi

≈ Fish with steamed vegetables and a side of fruit

≈ Tuna sandwich with mustard and lettuce

≈ For more healthy lunch choices visit my favorite health and wellness doctor, Dr. Andrew Weil at www.Drweil.com. He is the co-author of *Healthy Kitchen* and the author of *Eating Well for Optimum Health*.

EAT SMALLER, MORE FREQUENT MEALS

Research published in the "New England Journal of Medicine" recommends that we will benefit greatly if we eat smaller more frequent meals and spread out our food intake throughout the day rather than eating one or two large meals. According to Dan Benardot, Ph.D., R.D., associate dean of research for the College of Health and Human Sciences at Georgia State University in Atlanta, we should eat every three hours or so to stay satiated and energized. Studies show if you have moderate-size meals plus small between-meal snacks you increase your levels of energy and alertness. Without healthy snacks your blood sugar falls and you experience fatigue and tension. Just as we need to constantly feed a fire with moderate size pieces of wood, we also need to continually supply our internal furnace with food that can be turned into fuel. This keeps our metabolism going strong and steady.

Eating smaller, more frequent meals pushes our energy higher and keeps our mind sharper. With a constant supply of fuel for our mind and body, our memory is enhanced, we learn more and our performance excels. The keys are to choose healthy smaller meals and eat energizing snacks. Here are a few of my family's favorite snacks:

- ≈ A smoothie made with fresh fruit, yogurt, and ice
- ≈ A handful of raisins and nuts
- ≈ Whole grain bread with a piece of cheese
- ≈ A protein shake
- ≈ Vegetarian chili or soup
- ≈ A piece of fruit

≈ Whole wheat cracker with a little peanut butter
≈ Hummus, pita bread and vegetables

 ACTION STEPS

1. Plan your meal and snacks the night before.

2. When you are traveling or are driving around bring healthy snacks with you or else when you become hungry you will likely run into a convenience store and grab a bag of chips.

3. Eat raisins and nuts instead of chips and cookies.

4. Buy a fruit bowl for your office or home.

GIVE THE GIFT
OF ENERGY

Thousands of candles can be lighted from a single candle, and the life of the candle will not be shortened. Happiness never decreases by being shared.

BUDDHA

Every interaction we have with another person is an exchange of energy. Whether it's a handshake, a discussion, a chance meeting or a greeting of "hello," we share our energy with someone and receive their energy in return. During these exchanges we have the opportunity to share positive energy instead of negative energy. We have the opportunity to create more energy for everyone and ourselves rather than causing an energy deficit. Too often people feel like they have to hoard energy, money, the attention of others, the limelight and everything else that can be accumulated. Greed makes them want more, more, more. They want the biggest piece of the pie instead of making more pies. What these people don't realize is that energy wants to be shared. When energy is shared it never decreases. Just as two candle flames held together create a larger flame, two forces of positive energy working together create more energy for everyone. If you have ever been in a brainstorming session or laughed for hours with old friends you haven't seen in a while, you understand the powerful force of energy that is shared and created when we give the gift of energy.

The key is to think like an Energy Addict and give the gift of energy to everyone you meet, work with, live with and interact with. Just as energy can be contagious, energy can also be increased and multiplied. Energy Addicts don't hoard energy. They make more energy for everyone around them and ultimately themselves. Energy Addicts know the more energy they give the more they receive. They don't want a bigger piece of pie; they make the pie bigger. They make their families, organizations, companies and teams better by giving and sharing their energy. Women like my wife give so much energy to their families they make everyone's life better. People such as CEO Michael Dell, Oprah, NFL quarterback Brent Favre, Steven Speilberg, and author Cheryl Richardson excel in life because they give the gift of energy....and make us all better off.

 ACTION STEPS

1. Treat every interaction as an exchange of energy.

2. Identify three ways you can give the gift of your energy each day. For example you might write, "Become a mentor, smile and encourage others to succeed."

VALUE YOUR BODY

If you have your health you truly have everything.

JANICE GORDON

How much do you value your body? What is it worth to you? Ask a person in need of an organ transplant and they would say priceless. Ask a scientist or doctor and they would say "in the millions of dollars". If we are worth so much then why do so many of us value our body so little? We may think we put a high value on our body, yet many of our actions prove otherwise. When we value something we apply energy towards it. We spend the time to water our plants because we value them. We pet our dogs because we love them. We nurture our children because we treasure them. We read the stock section of the paper because we value our financial investment.

Unfortunately many of us take better care of our $20,000 cars than our priceless body. We don't exercise our million dollar body because we have to work 15 hours a day at our $60,000 a year job. We allow everything else to be more important than our health and then we wonder why we get sick, gain weight, lose sleep and get depressed. Our actions demonstrate that we value everything more than our health. In fact, we often don't value our body or treat it with respect until we have caused ourselves serious harm or are in danger from diseases such as cancer or heart disease. Only when our health is threatened do we put a significant value on it. Only when we are in danger of losing our health do we treasure it.

The good news is things can change. Values can change. Actions can change. Today we can begin to value our body more than we value anything else. We can invest our energy in our body and our health. No matter how busy we are, a 20 minute walk each day will pay incredible dividends. Eating more fruits, vegetables and whole grains will add years to our lives allowing for a longer return on our investment. Recharging your batteries each night with at least eight hours of sleep will make your investment operate optimally. Why shouldn't we do these things since our health is certainly more valuable than any mutual fund, any job or any project. And the best part of all is when you value your body more than anything else you will actually create more success in all the areas of your life. One of my grandmother's favorite sayings was "if you have your health you have everything." I certainly agree with her. When you value your body, your investment will provide you with everything you need for as long as you have it.

 ## ACTION STEPS

1. Write the following words on a piece of paper. "My body is worth millions of dollars."

2. Carry this paper with you in your pocket and look at it once a day.

3. Or in your calendar or date book, write "My body is worth millions of dollars."

4. In your check book write the same thing. This way you will remind yourself to invest your energy in your self as much as everything else.

TAKE SHORT
ENERGY BREAKS

The best know how to rest.

ALAN COHEN

Just as athletes need to take water breaks, now more than ever, in today's fast paced, 24/7, don't-stop-till-you-drop culture, we need to take short energy breaks to survive and thrive. Too often we push our mind and bodies to the max without regard for rest or sleep. Family life and career life ask more and more of us, requiring us to ask more and more of ourselves. We often tell ourselves we'll take a break when we're done with the latest house project or the newest business deal. We say we'll relax when the holidays are here or when school is out. The problem is that it's not going to get any easier. Life will continue to get more demanding and the demands on our time will continue to grow. Our energy will continue to decrease if we don't adapt. We can't change society so we have to change ourselves.

We have to take short energy breaks during our busy day. We must find the calm in the midst of chaos because the question is if not then, when? The best thing about an energy break is it doesn't have to be a long time. Dr. Etienne Grandjean, a productivity expert at the Swiss Polytechnic Institute, has studied human performance and he suggests that people who take short breaks have a greater number of total accomplishments per day and exhibit less distress and fatigue. Short breaks also contribute to an increase in energy for an entire morning or afternoon. If you are not sure when to take a break, look for the following signs.

≈ You can't focus and concentrate.
≈ You are starving.
≈ You body feels stiff.
≈ You feel anxious and shaky.
≈ You can't keep your eyes open.

Also, as a general rule try to take a short break every 90 to 120 minutes. Once you decide you need a short break then it is important to do something that will energize you when your break is over. Here are a few action steps you can take during your energy break.

 ACTION STEPS

1. If you work in an office, stand up and stretch at your desk or go outside and stretch and loosen up your shoulders.

2. If you are home take a walk around the block. Or go to the park and connect with nature.

3. Find a restroom sink and splash cold water on your face.

4. Eat a healthy snack.

5. Close your eyes and focus on your breathing.

6. Get a drink of water or green tea.

7. Visit with a colleague or neighbor and share a story or a joke.

8. Call your significant other.

PAUSE FOR MORE ENERGY

In my seminars I say that there is a disease inflicting Americans in epidemic proportions. It's called But stickitis totheseatis. Many of our jobs now require us to sit in chairs for hours upon hours a day. We sit so long we have to almost peel ourselves from the chair in order to get up. For our energy's sake research says that this is not a good thing. Studies show that when we work for longer than 20 to 30 minutes straight on a single task, the time we need for the problem solving increases by up to 500 percent, according to Dr. Etienne Grandjean. Therefore a task that could only take 10 minutes will take 50 minutes to complete instead. Given that many of us spend hours in front of a computer screen or working at a desk without moving, we can clearly see the need for a solution.

Thankfully, my favorite business and management expert, Dr. Robert K. Cooper, recommends a solution he calls "the strategic pause." The strategic pause only requires 30-60 seconds and will produce 30 minutes of active-energy boosting. The strategic pause is similar to an energy break, just shorter. Dr. Cooper suggests we pause every 30 minutes from the activity we are doing. If you're typing, pause. If you're researching online, pause. If you're reading a book for longer than 30 minutes, pause. Dr. Grandjean's studies suggest pauses, for as little as 30 to 60 seconds, actually speed up work and increase energy by up to 100 percent or more for the next half-hour. Dr. Cooper states, "With each brief pause, you do more than refresh your mind and invigorate your senses and stamina. You also send a series of simple yet powerful signals to your brain and senses about how alive you want to feel and how active you want to be." In reading this you are probably asking, "OK, pauses are good but how do I pause? What's in a pause?" Dr. Cooper recommends the following action steps to incorporate into your energy pauses. These steps, when done every 30 minutes, will produce hours of increased energy. I know; I do them often and they helped me when I was writing this book.

 ACTION STEPS

1. Shift your gaze. Give your eyes a break by looking at something else. If you stare at a computer screen all day, look away. Look at the window. Stand up and look across the room.

2. Sip ice water. With each sip you increase your energy and alertness.

3. Get some bright light. Many people report that when they're exposed to bright sunlight they experience a strong sense of calmness followed by a surge of energy. Even indoor light can increase your energy.

4. Breathe. Take the 10 energizing breaths I discussed earlier in the book

5. Stretch. Get the blood and energy moving through your body.

EXERCISE: MAKE IT SIMPLE

If exercise could be packaged into a pill, it would be the single most prescribed and beneficial medicine in the nation.

ROBERT BUTLER, M.D. MOUNT SINAI MEDICAL CENTER

There is a lot of well-documented evidence that supports the claim exercise reduces stress, increases energy and makes people healthier. However, we don't really need anyone to tell us working out is good for us when we know first hand from our own experiences and feelings. When we take a jog and break a sweat, we feel good. When we talk a long walk and get our blood pumping through our bodies we feel energized. We may feel a little sore the next day if we haven't exercised in a while, but the soreness quickly subsides and is replaced by strength and power. Exercise helps us build muscle and reduce fat. It clears our minds, reduces our stress, strengthens our heart and energizes our lives. Research shows that exercise is equal to antidepressants for mild and moderate depression. After an exercise session, we have a positive outlook on the world and believe that we can take on anything.

If you're like me, exercise helps you put all of the little annoying life problems, that otherwise would consume you, into perspective. For instance, my wife is always worried about paying the bills, calling the gas company, getting our daughter new clothes for school, finding a babysitter for Saturday night and a thousand other nuisances. However, when she goes to the gym, she returns worry-free, with a feeling that everything will work out just fine. When she feels this way, strangely enough, it always does.

We know what the experts say. We know how we feel when we work out. What's stopping us then? Why don't we stand up and do it more often? Are we too busy? I believe the answer is no. Most of us don't exercise enough because we make exercise too complicated. We think we have to follow strict programs and lift weights five days a week to be effective. While I believe exercise programs are great for a number of people, I also believe life today makes it difficult for a majority of people to follow strict and rigid exercise programs. Just the other day, I was talking to a friend who said he didn't have time to exercise today because it took so long to get to the gym. I told him exercise doesn't need to take place in a gym to be effective. We don't need expensive equipment or spin classes. All we need is a pair of shoes and a place to walk.

The key to increased energy is to make exercise simple. If there is time to get to the gym, then let's go to the gym. If we only have 30 minutes, let's walk around the block or take a bike ride. If we are traveling on business or visiting family, let's walk around the city. If we are staying in a hotel and it's raining let's walk up and down the stairs for 20 minutes. Simply exercising for five to 20 minutes will increase your energy and provide substantial health benefits. While exercising one hour is better than 10 minutes, if 10 minutes is all you have then 10 minutes is what you should do. The best exercise is the one that you will do. Here are a few action steps to help you make exercise simple.

ACTION STEPS

1. Commit to doing one form of exercise six days a week.

2. Determine what form of exercise is available to you on any given day. Walking? Biking? Gym? Yoga? Other?

3. Decide what exercise you are going to do the night before. Planning helps you stick to your commitment.

4. Determine what time you are going to exercise based on your schedule. Decide how much time you have to exercise.

5. Vary your exercise routine so you don't get bored. Walk one day. If you belong to a gym go to the gym the next day. Ride your bike the next. Play basketball. Play tag with your kids.

6. Make it fun. Wear headphones if you walk on a treadmill. Listen to your favorite music or audio book.

7. Remember the purpose of exercise. To increase your energy and improve your health. If you keep it simple, exercise will always be an energizing part of your life.

8. Visit author and trainer Michael Gerrish at www.exerciseplus.com. He is a great resource for achieving your fitness goals. Also read his book, *The Mind-Body Makeover Project*.

FORGIVE

Holding on to anger is like grasping a hot coal with the intent of throwing it at someone else; you are the one getting burned.

BUDDHA

One of the great lessons in life is to learn the practice of forgiveness. When we hold onto resentments and negative feelings about people who have hurt, betrayed, or misled us we literally allow this negative energy to fill us up. It weighs us down like a ton of bricks and stops positive energy from flowing into our lives. Sure, it's normal to get upset at first but the problems occur when we hold on too long to our negative feelings and emotions. Like a snake bite, it's not that bite that kills us, but rather the venom in our blood and veins that does us in. Resentment and anger represent the venom and negative energy that can poison our lives if we let them.

When I was a young boy, my father and mother divorced. My father remarried and his new family became his number one priority. As is the case with many divorced families, people get hurt and in this case my brother and I were the ones most affected. As I grew up, the feelings of anger and resentment began to build within me. Angry because he was not there when we needed him. Resentful of the fact his new family always came first and his sons came last. This anger and resentment persisted well into adulthood. I moved away from home and had not seen my father for nine years. We didn't speak. He didn't come to my wedding. Life went on. Then one day after a conversation with my brother, I realized how angry I still was. I realized how this resentment was filling me up. I knew I could never be all that I could be without letting go of this hate.

So, that day I simply decided to forgive. I called him up; he admitted where he made mistakes and I understood how tough it must have been to being pulled in two different directions. My daughter and I visited him a month later and I felt like a weight had been lifted off my shoulders.

When you forgive, remember, you are not doing it for the person you are forgiving. You are doing if for yourself. Dr. Wayne Dyer likes to talk about the Chinese proverb that says when you pursue revenge you must build two graves: one for them and one for yourself. No one benefits when you hold anger and hate inside you. However, when you let go and forgive you will be the one who benefits most. When you forgive you allow more peace, love, joy and other sources of positive energy into your life. You clear out the bad energy and replace it with the good. You stop being a victim and you start taking control of your own life and happiness. You don't let others dictate how you feel, rather, you choose your attitude. If someone upsets you, betrays you or hurts you, allow yourself to get upset momentarily and then let the negative energy go. Just as you get an oil change for your car, you need to clear out the sludge that is preventing you from operating at peak performance.

 ACTION STEPS

1. Decide who you need to forgive.

2. Say "I forgive (the person's name) for doing (what)." Forgive with your words and forgive with your heart. Release your anger and resentment.

3. If the person is alive call them up and tell them that you forgive them. Don't expect a certain response. Remember you are forgiving for you, not for them. If they don't appreciate your forgiveness, don't let this stop you from forgiving.

4. Also keep in mind that just because you forgive someone doesn't mean they have to be in your life. While you
may forgive someone for their past indiscretion, you are
not forced to be their best friend now or in the future.

5. You may need to forgive a person who is no longer living. Many times we hold on to anger and resentment long
after someone dies. In this case, do action steps one and
two. If it helps you can also write a letter of forgiveness.

TAKE A WALK
AFTER LUNCH

*The higher your energy level, the more efficient your body. The more
efficient your body, the better you feel and the more you
will use your talent to produce outstanding results.*

ANTHONY ROBBINS

Do you often feel like collapsing into a big chair and taking a
nap after lunch? You sit at your desk or on your couch at
home trying to fight the urge to fall asleep. You feel as unproductive as a plumber without a wrench. Now, research tells
us there is a great way to add more energy to our day.
Walking for five to 10 minutes after lunch can greatly
increase our energy for the rest of the day. While eating a
healthy moderate sized lunch will give us energy, walking
after lunch will multiply the energy boosting effect of food.
When we exercise after lunch we burn even more calories
and produce even more energy for our body.

Robert E. Thayer, Ph. D., professor of biological psychology at California State University, found that as little as 10
minutes of brisk walking leads to very significant increases
in energy. However, we don't need studies to tell us how an
after lunch walk makes us feel. Just try it for a few weeks
and you will be able to do your own personal study. The best
thing about my energy tips is that you can try them immediately and see if they work for you. You can decide what you
want to incorporate into your life by putting my tips to the
test. One of the first experiments you should try is walking
after lunch since I believe it will be one of your biggest
sources of increased energy in the afternoon.

When I read the research on walking after lunch, I did my
own tests and found that even a light walk energized me and
helped me be more productive after lunch and throughout

the afternoon. I continue the practice till this day. While I often become hungry sooner because of the increase in calories and fuel I am burning, I find it is better to be hungry sooner than sluggish and tired. To compensate for this hunger, I simply eat an energizing snack (included on page 65) which keeps me even more alert until dinner. To help you put the habit of walking after lunch into practice I have listed a few Action Steps.

 ACTION STEPS

1. If you go out to lunch, park far enough away from the restaurant so you have to take a light walk to and from your car.

2. If your office is near restaurants, walk to and from lunch. Or drive with a friend and walk back.

3. Create a walking group in your office to walk around the office after lunch. One of my co-workers did this in Atlanta and people loved it.

4. If you are at home during lunch, walk around your block or hop on a treadmill.

ENERGY BUILDING

At this point in the book you may realize there are several actions you can take during the midday that when done together will greatly increase your energy in the afternoon. I call this practice "energy building" because you build your life with one energy source at a time that when added together make a big difference. Like a ladder, consider each new habit as a rung that will take your energy one step higher. When you make time for lunch (page 61), eat a healthy energizing lunch (page 63) walk after lunch, and eat an energizing snack (page 65) you provide your body will real fuel instead of needing candy bars and coffee to get you through the day. I call this the beginning of the end of fake energy dependency. You will find as you change your habits, you change your energy and you change your life.

Energy building is all about selecting a few of the tips suggested in this book and incorporating them into your life one at a time. As you add each habit to your life you will see your energy increase higher and higher. The key is to take small steps rather than trying to do too much at once. We don't want anyone to create an energy overload and blowout their power plant. Make one or at most a few tips a habit at a time and then add another energy tip. With each action you will build your life and increase your energy.

Energy building can be done with various energy sources. Exercising in the morning (page 19), eating breakfast (page 51), and starting your day with positive thoughts (page 105) will help you create a more energetic and productive morning. Eating a snack before dinner (page 65), eating a light and healthy dinner (page 65), and walking after dinner (page 83) will fuel your night time with more energy, more fun and happiness. Remember, you don't need to do everything in this book. Simply decide what works for you, practice energy building, and watch your energy soar.

One of my clients simply put three of my tips into practice and lost weight, noticed increased energy, and became a motivator to her employees and family. My client and her daughter now take after dinner walks allowing them to spend more time together and live more energetically.

 ACTION STEPS

1. Decide what tips you are going to incorporate into your life.

2. Incorporate one or at most a few habits at a time.

3. Observe how your energy increases.

4. Please email me your results. Jon@jongordon.com.

MASTER THE FLOW
OF MONEY

Once and for all let's break down money into its most basic form and give it the status it deserves. Money is not a god and should not be worshiped like one. Money, in itself, is not powerful, but it can be used in powerful ways. Money is a form of energy simply waiting to be transformed, exchanged, saved and used, with its power derived from what it can be turned into. The food we buy, the vacations we take, the lifestyle we live.

Money, like all forms of energy, is used differently by different people. Jamie needs a lot to live. Judy uses very little. Jack takes in a lot and expends a lot. Kathy conserves most of what she takes in. Money can be a friend who helps build a life or it can become an enemy that knocks us down. If you have ever been in or known someone in serious debt, you understand the magnitude of this statement. When used properly, money can provide us with the life we have always wanted or it can make our world a living nightmare.

Once we simplify how we think about money, we can simplify how we use money in our life. When the public uses more electricity than the power companies produce, we call this a power crisis—an energy deficit. The same can be said for a person who spends more energy than they make. Eventually the deficit grows and a personal crisis results. To master the flow of money, you must master the flow of the energy of money. An energy crisis will not occur if we apply one simple rule to our life.

Spend only what you have. Or don't spend it if you don't have it. I know this sounds so simple you're wondering why I'm stating the obvious. My answer is that we often overlook the obvious. This is because we are constantly being attacked by confusing programs, advertisements and financial instruments that complicate our view of money. From "consolidated lines of credit" to "low-interest credit cards" to "no payments for

180 days" clauses—its easy to lose our way. Millions of Americans are in debt because of one thing. They spend more than they make. The law of energy says if you spend energy you don't have, then you will need to find that energy somewhere else. Usually it's in the form of a credit card or loan. Eventually you spend your life trying to replenish the borrowed energy rather than accumulating energy for future needs. If you get to the point where you can't even replenish your borrowed energy, an energy crisis could become a power plant shut down. The key is to not let the meter go past empty. If input is light then output needs to be cut back. Whatever the sacrifice, the flow of energy must be balanced and the outflow of money should only increase when inflow increases.

 ACTION STEPS

1. Think of money as energy.

2. Identify how you currently use money. Is it your friend or enemy? Does it control you or do you control it?

3. Determine your current monthly inflow (income) and outflow (expenses). Do you spend more than you take in?

4. If your expenses exceed your income, reduce your expenses so that your inflow is more than your outflow.

5. Determine what expenses you can reduce and by how much.

6. Read *The Wall Street Journal Guide to Understanding Money & Investing* by Kenneth M. Morris. It will help you understand all of the different methods of investing.

7. Visit www.fool.com or www.clarkhoward.com for more information on financial matters and ways to save money.

BUILD MORE POWER PLANTS

Wealth flows from energy and ideas.

WILLIAM FEATHER

While I don't believe that money can buy you happiness I do recognize that money is energy and if you create more money you create more energy. This energy can be used to improve your health or to improve the lives of others. It can be used to take a trip to the beach or visit relatives in another state. When we don't allow ourselves to become attached to money we can enjoy having it and spending it. While money can't buy you happiness, happy people can do a lot of great things with money. Money, like all forms of energy, can be used to exchange positive energy. So I suggest you build some power plants, make some money and exchange it for the things that you want. Just remember. Money can't be exchanged for happiness, love or true success.

In life, we realize that when it comes to money, there are those who search for energy and those who create it. We have a choice. We can either dig for coal and fight to pay off our debts or we can build more power plants. My friend Corey decided to be an energy creator. He knew it was time to find other ways to make money besides his weekly paycheck. He bought a condominium with money he had saved over the last few years, fixed it up and rented it for more than his monthly mortgage. This one act increased his flow of money by $2,400 a year. After a few years he had saved enough money to buy another condo. He now had two power plants producing energy. Within a year he bought a third rental property. Then he sold one of his properties and used the profits to buy a more expensive condo that produced more energy. When I last checked Corey had five income producing power plants that added over $25,000 a year to his yearly input.

Keep in mind that I use Corey's example only to demonstrate how one person created their power plants. While real estate came easy to Corey, it may not suit your personality, skill or schedule. The key is to determine what power plants you want to build and then build them. Save more money than you spend. Then invest in a company. Buy a rental property. Place your money in a bank CD. Open a mutual fund. Start a business. For me, I found that restaurants were my power plants. Two years ago I decided to open a restaurant that would support my writing and speaking efforts. I now have three restaurants - or three power plants producing energy. I always lose money in stocks. I am not very good with real estate. But I know how to make money in restaurants. They work for me and you have to decide what works for you. I suggest you build power plants that you know how to manage. Then grow them. Then multiply them. Over the years your power plants will provide you with money for life.

 ACTION STEPS

1. Read *Rich Dad, Poor Dad* by Robert T. Kiyosaki. This book really did change my life.

2. Determine what power plants you want to build.

3. Save your money and start putting money towards these power plants.

4. When you make money from one power plant use this money to build another power plant or a bigger power plant.

REMEMBER, IT'S NOT A RACE

I found myself saying this to my daughter the other day and when I said it I knew I had to share with you a story about how I went from rushing to cruising.

Before I met my wife I was always rushing; rushing to get to the store, rushing to reach my goals, rushing through life hoping to get there faster. While I have learned a lot about life from my wife, the biggest lesson I have learned from her is the practice of cruising. Like a car in cruise control, my wife goes at her own steady pace. She eats her meals slowly, savoring each bite. She does the dishes on her own time, not my time. She never rushes to get things done but always manages to get everything done—on her time—at her pace.

While I used to view her way as slow and unproductive, which you can imagine led to many arguments, I grew to realize that she knew a secret that I didn't. Instead of letting society and other people, including me, rush her, she dictated her own pace. If the kids would oversleep for school, she wouldn't panic and rush them 90 mph to school as I would have. Instead she would simply bring them 30 minutes late and believe it or not, life still went on. The sun still set, the school didn't fall down and the kids still learned their alphabet. I realized rushing really doesn't get things done quicker. While we may move faster or fidget more, we don't make up that much time to call rushing a productivity tool. In fact research states that rushing leads to more mistakes and stress, causing us to work more. Rushing is also a main cause of energy drain.

Just as we use more gas when we try to weave in and out of cars to get to our destination faster, we also expend more personal energy when we rush. We spend so much energy rushing around we don't have any left when we get there.

It's like rushing to a vacation and not being able to enjoy it or rushing to receive a promotion and not being able to perform because of burnout. In contrast, when you put your life on cruise control you'll find that you'll have more energy every leg of the trip. You'll have more energy to accomplish your short-term tasks and long-term goals. When you cruise instead of rush you still get things done but without the panic and stress.

Cruising works and rushing doesn't because life really isn't a race. And when you think about it, if life was a race, would you really want to win? Wouldn't that mean you would just go through life faster than everyone else, enjoying less, seeing less and doing less? Like rushing through an amusement park you really wouldn't get to enjoy the full experience. I often tell people at my seminars that if you continue to think life is a race, consider that the stress, frustration and depression associated with rushing just might push you to the finish line faster than all of your family and friends. Would you really want to win this kind of race?

 ACTION STEPS

1. When you find your self rushing:

≈ Say to yourself "Life isn't a race."

≈ Take several deep breaths and relax.

≈ Pay attention to where you are and what you are doing now rather than thinking about what has to be done and where you have to be.

≈ Say to yourself, "I have the time to get everything done that I need to get done. Everything always works out when I don't rush."

≈ Make this a habit. If you practice these techniques often they will become part of who you are. You will become a cruiser instead of a rusher.

THE ENERGY OF
"THANK YOU"

If the only prayer you say in your life is "thank you," that would suffice.

MEISTER ECKHART

Being thankful has changed my life and the energy of "thank you" is one of my most powerful sources of energy. Over the last few years I have learned that there is so much to be thankful for and the more we thank the more energy we bring into our lives. When we say "thank you" and feel thankful we focus the energy of our minds, words and hearts on what we have rather than what we don't. This energy allows us to be more present, focusing our energy on the "now" rather than the "future" or negative events of the "past." Being thankful gives you inner peace because you appreciate what you have rather than always wanting something more. Where, in the past, I would always ask God for things but never thank God for them, I now thank God for everything in my life. The "thank you's" can be general. "Thank you for my health and the health of my children." "Thank you for my wife and my home." "Thank you for food on my table." They can also be specific. "Thank you for my friends Brian and Ted." "Thank you for a healthy knee that allows me to play basketball." "Thank you that my children have the voices to wake me up in the morning even if I'm not happy about it."

The energy of "thank you" can change your entire life. My friend Jeff told me a story about how when he arrived home from work, his wife sent him unwillingly to the grocery store. On the drive to the store he couldn't stop fuming with angry thoughts and words not fit for this book. Yet, on the way home, he remembered "thank you." He thanked God for the car that took him to the grocery store. He thanked God for the money to buy food. He thanked God for a wife who needed him to buy groceries. By the time he arrived home he was even thankful for the legs to walk and carry six bags of groceries up and down three flights of stairs. When he walked into the door he and his wife embraced, kissed and life was good. Two simple words changed his outlook on life, his internal energy and the energy he projected out into the world.

In addition to inner peace, practicing gratitude also attracts more positive people, things and events into our lives. As in Jeff's case, when you are thankful you vibrate with positive energy and you project this positive energy into the world. Like a magnet, positive people and other forms of energy are attracted to you. It's ironic that by being thankful you actually attract more positive energy in your life than by asking. But that's the way energy works and each day you have the power to make the energy of "thank you" work for you. Just say "thank you" with your words and feel it with your "heart."

 ACTION STEPS

1. Say "thank you" to people whenever you get a chance.

2. Write thank you notes or thank you e-mails.

3. Whenever you feel stressed, annoyed or unhappy, remember "thank you."

4. In the morning and before you go to bed, tell God what you are thankful for.

5. Identify 3 people you would like to thank today and call them or write them.

EAT MORE EARLIER

Eat breakfast like a king, lunch like a prince, and dinner like a pauper.

ADELLE DAVIS

One of the simple keys to increased energy is to eat a majority of your calories earlier in the day rather than later in the evening. According to one preliminary study, R. Curtis Ellison, M.D., a scientist at Boston University School of Medicine, showed that compared to French men and women who consume 57 percent of their daily calories before 2:00 pm and are very active in the evening, Americans take in a total of 38 percent of their daily calories before 2:00 pm. And as many of us know, most Americans eat large dinner meals and often stumble over to the couch to watch television until bedtime. So what effect does eating a majority of our calories earlier in the day have on our bodies and energy? Consider the following study.

According to Robert K. Cooper, PhD, author of *High Energy Living*, in a study conducted at the University of Minnesota, researchers compared groups of people on 2,000-calorie-a-day diets to find out which groups had the most energy and lost the most weight. The study showed people who ate earlier in the day had the most energy and lost weight. People on the same diet who consumed most of their calories later in the day gained weight and felt most tired. In addition to increased energy the difference in weight loss was also amazing. The people who ate more calories earlier lost an average of 2.3 more pounds per week.

To help you eat more calories earlier in the day, here are

a few Action Steps. Some of these Action Steps are so impor-tant I wrote a complete section on them.

 ACTION STEPS

1. Eat a healthy and satisfying breakfast.

2. Eat energizing snacks throughout the day for increased energy.

3. Try not to eat dinner past 7 pm. Ideally try to eat before 6 pm.

4. Eat smaller meals but more of them. Instead of two or three large meals eat three meals and two snacks.

5. On weekends eat your main meal at midday.

STRAIGHTEN UP

Did you know that poor posture can reduce the amount of oxygen you take in to your lungs by 30 percent or more? This means less oxygen for your body and brain and less energy for you. Much of the research also suggests poor posture affects more than just your oxygen intake. It also influences the way you feel, think and act. According to Rene Cailliet, M.D., chairman of the department of physical medicine at the Santa Monica Hospital Center, when you're stooped over, you not only look old and out of touch with life but you also tend to feel that way. Now we know why Mom always said "straighten up."

Dr. Cailliet's claim is not surprising when we think about how we feel when we walk straight with our head up. We also can observe the body language of others to see the relationship between posture and attitude. Think of two people. One walks slouched over. He is timid. He always sits slouched over. He seems unsure and indecisive. You almost don't want to look at him because you might scare him. Then think of the other person. She walks tall. She has a bounce to her demeanor, even sitting at her desk. She carries herself with confidence and she stands out for the right reasons.

Experts know and we know from our experiences and observations that the link between our posture and attitude is bi-directional. Posture can affect your attitude, just as attitude affects your posture. I consider this great news since science is telling us that we have one more tool to improve our attitude and increase our energy. If you want to make improvements one of the places to start is how you sit and stand. As many of us know, in a technology driven world this is not an easy task but it can be done. Many of our jobs require us to sit at a desk looking at a computer screen all day. Many of us have become inflicted with a 21st century disease I call *Head Forwarditis*—where we are always leaning forward with our shoulders and following with our head. With each forward slouch we're cutting the supply of oxygen to our lungs, decreasing our energy and affecting our attitude.

Thankfully, the solution is clear. If we pay attention to our posture and focus on standing and sitting up straight we can make significant changes in how we feel and think. Posture expert Wilfred Barlow, M.D., says "We're not born knowing how to do it right...we have to learn it." No matter our height, we can practice sitting tall, walking tall and thinking tall. We can "straighten up" for increased energy.

 ACTION STEPS

1. Practice standing and sitting up straight as much as possible.

2. Make it a habit to focus on your posture every 30 minutes. Eventually great posture will feel natural.

3. When you are feeling sad or upset, pay even more attention to your posture. Force yourself to "straighten up."

STOP LOOKING AT THE COMPUTER SCREEN

Let's face it, human beings were not meant to sit at a desk for 12 hours a day looking at a computer screen. Think about that for a second. Our evolutionary history tells us we were hunters and gatherers. Searching for food. Walking, running, lifting, carrying. Then we moved to an agrarian society. We farmed. We milked cows, chopped wood, and worked the land. Moving forward we progressed to an industrial society. We worked the machines, lifted boxes and supplies, and used physical labor to manufacture goods. Now at the dawn of the information age we move ideas, exchange information, create new business models, program code and create websites.

Sure, there is a physical side to the information age in the distribution and fulfillment of e-commerce, but the only real exercise a technology business requires of 90 percent of its workforce is having them walk through the airport or lift a server. The creator of Dilbert became famous for depicting and making fun at the daily life of an office worker which consists mostly of working at one's desk, on the computer, looking at the computer screen. For many of us, it is no laughing matter because we work in an office. We may break for a meeting but then it's back to the desk. Time to get something to eat. Then back to the desk to either read or write or code or e-mail or think. It's not our fault. That is what a job in the information age entails. Our job description didn't read, "must be able to lift and operate heavy machinery or must be able to milk cows and cut down trees." Our job requires us to use our knowledge and mental skills and to work at a computer. This is not a bad thing. It is simply the reality today—and more people will continue to be added to this category.

We shouldn't have to quit our jobs and join the Peace Corps or go to Montana to work on a farm to become more active. Instead we can get up once in a while and stop looking at the computer screen. We can be more active when we are not working and we can do certain things at the office to keep from going stir crazy. We can adapt.

We can take a walk around the office and talk to someone in another department. In addition to taking a break, we just might share some valuable knowledge with each other. We can go outside and sit on a bench or even the ground, and get some fresh air. We can go sit somewhere quiet and close our eyes and meditate. No matter what we do, we need to realize that our desk is not a prison and our computer is not the warden. There are times when we have to get up, break free and spread our wings. So the next time you feel like it's one of those times, don't even hesitate. Just get up and stop looking at the computer screen. You deserve a break.

 ACTION STEPS

1. Write down the times during your day that you can take a short break.

2. At first, schedule short breaks from your computer. Eventually it will become a habit.

BELIEVE THAT MIRACLES HAPPEN EVERY DAY

There are only two ways to live your life. One is as though nothing is a miracle. The other is as though everything is a miracle.

ALBERT EINSTEIN

When we choose to believe that everything is a miracle, suddenly our life opens up to a world of possibilities. Our entire state of being changes. Our mood lightens and our energy soars. Like a new pair of glasses we see the world differently and this view changes the way we think and feel. Instead of a baby we see the birth of a miracle. Instead of a child we see unlimited potential. A simple flower becomes another example of God's amazing creations. Obstacles become hurdles to success. Negative past experiences become learning experiences. Potential energy becomes boundless energy.

A belief in miracles is a belief that anything is possible. Any goal is achievable. Wishes are granted and dreams come true. When you believe in miracles you work that much harder with that much more passion and energy because you know it can and will be done. Your belief in miracles awakens your hidden genius and unleashes your awesome potential. You tap your potential energy and transform each miracle into actual energy. While the doubters close themselves off to the energy of all possibilities your belief in miracles attracts energy to you in order to create the possible. Energy wants to be used and if you have the will, the energy of what's possible will help you find a way.

A belief in miracles is also a belief that everything happens for a reason. A friend of mine recently said to me, "A coincidence is when God chooses to remain anonymous." I love this quote because I have always believed there are no accidents. Everything is a miracle. Each event, each lesson, each person has been placed in our life for a reason. When we believe in miracles we see the divinity in everything. All designed to help us become better people. To grow. To learn. God doesn't need to take the credit because when we believe everything is a miracle, we give credit where credit is due. A chance meeting. A right turn instead of a left, a near accident, or cancer in remission are all signs that miracles happen every day. If you choose to believe in miracles, they will happen to you and your life will be filled with incredible energy.

 ACTION STEPS

1. Read the book *Small Miracles: Extraordinary Coincidences from Everyday Life*, by Yitta Halberstam and Judith Leventhal.

2. Remember any past miracles that have happened in your life. Write them down.

3. Think about the current miracles in your life. Write them down.

4. Ask friends and family to share any miracles that have happened in their lives.

TWO POWER SOURCES ARE BETTER THAN ONE

The strategy of "energy combining" has long been one of my most successful habits for increased energy during busy times. In today's world, with so much to do and only 24 hours in a day, it is extremely effective to tap two of your power sources, we have discussed in this book, at the same time. For example, when I ride the exercise bike at the gym I often will read an inspirational book. Instead of an hour of reading at night and an hour of bicycling in the morning I accomplish both tasks in one hour and create more energy in less time. With each peddle and word read, I tap two power sources instead of just one. I also like to walk on the beach in the morning and pray while I walk. Walking energizes my mind and body. Praying energizes my spirit. When I am finished, I feel completely energized.

Energy combining can be done with a number of your power sources. You can walk on a treadmill and talk to a good friend. With each step and word you energize yourselves and each other. You can listen to your favorite audio book while you drive to work. Or you can play with your kids and connect with nature by visiting parks together. The combinations are endless. All you need to do is decide what power sources you want to incorporate into your life. Then just determine which power sources can be incorporated effectively at the same time. With each successful energy combination you'll find your energy increase exponentially and efficiently as you tap more power sources in less time.

ACTION STEPS

1. Write down two power sources you can incorporate into your life at the same time.

2. Sometime this week, take action and practice energy combining.

START YOUR DAY
OFF RIGHT

When you arise in the morning, think of what a precious privilege it is to be alive—to breathe, to think, to enjoy, to love.

MARCUS AURELIUS

Did you know that researchers can predict what your energy levels will be like in the afternoon by knowing what you do in the morning? A new client of mine called me up the other day and said, "I always crash in the afternoon. What can I do?" I said to him, "I bet you hit the snooze button a few times. Jump out of bed. Rush to the shower. Gulp a cup of coffee and rush out the door. While sitting in your car you realize you forgot to get dressed. You rush back in the house, get dressed, and rush back to your car. You yell at a few people for driving slowly on the road. Get to your desk. You have e-mails in your inbox and voicemails you have not returned. The day starts and you're tired already. You grab a cup of coffee and now you're ready to begin the day. " He said, "That's me. How did you know?" I told him that many people start the day off like this and a bad start is one of the key contributing factors to fatigue in the afternoon. It also contributes to a larger problem in our lives I call the vicious cycle which I address on page 49.

When we spend our morning rushing around, our bodies run on stress hormones instead of "real energy." Stress hormones send flight-or-fight responses through your system causing you to have more energy temporarily. Like a person in a fight, energy increases dramatically. However, if you have ever been in a fight, you know afterwards your energy is drained and you feel exhausted. The problem is that stress hormones only work for a short period of time—most likely a trait developed through evolution to ensure our survival in the short term. Whether it's a fight or a fight to start the day, your stress hormones will give you energy now but cause you to crash later.

The key to increased energy is to start your day off right and fuel your morning with your sustained power sources instead of stress hormones. Starting your day off right is like warming up your car on a freezing winter morning. When you warm it up everything runs much better. Each day you make a choice about how much energy you will have in the afternoon by what you do in the morning.

If your choice is to increase your metabolism and have more energy then you might want to try the following action steps.

ACTION STEPS

1. Awake to music instead of a beeping alarm. Researchers say this helps you awake more peacefully instead of shocking your body and brain out of sleep. Keep the volume high enough to wake you but not so high that it startles you.

2. Don't hit the snooze button. Give yourself enough time to engage in an energizing morning instead of having to rush around.

3. Breathe. When you get out of bed take a few energizing breaths as discussed on page 29.

4. Drink water. This will refuel your body with water lost during your sleep.

5. Find the light. Many studies report that when we expose our body and brain to bright light we increase our alertness and energy. When you turn on a lamp in the

morning, go to a window, or walk outside the light helps you get ready to take on the day.

6. Think positive thoughts. Think positively about the day ahead and you increase your mental and physical energy. Instead of being fearful and anxious, causing a release of stress hormones, thinking positively about the day will send positive energy to your body supplying you with sustained energy.

7. Get inspired. Start your day with a positive quote. Instead of reading the latest news of killings, rapes and scandals, read something that energizes you. Perhaps it's a quote book, or *Simple Abundance* or the Bible.

8. Exercise. (page 75) When you exercise even just five minutes in the morning you kick start your metabolism which sets you up for increased energy during the day.

9. Eat breakfast (page 51). Where stress hormones will cause you to crash, a healthy breakfast will set you up for success every day. Follow breakfast with an energizing lunch and you are on your way to conquering the vicious cycle.

Just remember, from the moment you wake up you are dictating how much energy you will have during the day. With each activity, you choose to increase your metabolism, your energy and your health. A great start to the day results in a great day.

BE ACTIVE

If not now, When?

THE TALMUD

When we think of exercise we often think of putting on our exercise clothes, stretching, and making the sweat pour out of the body. However, there are many great ways to energize our mind and bodies that don't take a lot of time and don't require a lot of planning. These activities help you BE ACTIVE. They get your body in motion. They make you move a little more and get the energy circulating through your body. Our bodies were not meant to sit at desks and couches all day. They were meant to walk, move, run, and be active. While many of us don't have a choice of what we do on company time, we do have a choice to be active on our time. Here are a few action steps to help you choose to BE ACTIVE.

ACTION STEPS

1. Take the stairs at work instead of the elevator.

2. Park in the farthest row from the grocery store.

3. Take a short walk after lunch and dinner.

4. Instead of letting your dog hang out in the backyard take her for a walk.

5. If it's not far away, ride your bike to the grocery store

for a few needed items.

6. Walk and talk with your kids or grandkids after dinner.

7. Stand up and stretch throughout the day.

8. Do some yard work.

9. Help clean up the house.

10. Put on some music and dance by yourself or with your significant other.

11. Jump rope for two to three minutes.

12. If you are a new mom, take your child for walks in a baby stroller or jogger.

13. Swim with your kids on the weekends.

14. When you go to get your mail, take a two-minute walk while you're outside.

15. Play tennis and golf.

16. Take a water aerobics class at your local health club or YMCA.

FIND THE LIGHT

Have you ever stood outside for a few minutes and felt your body soaking up the sun like a solar panel fueling up with energy? Or felt more energized after spending some time outdoors?

Well, scientists now tell us, there is link between exposure to light and our energy levels. In a three-year study conducted at Harvard University, Drs. Richard Kronauer and Charles Czeisler were able to link the impact of light on the retina of the eye to better attention focus and energy production in the brain. According to Dr. Robert Cooper, other studies have shown that the body has hundreds of biochemical and hormonal rhythms, all keyed to light and dark, and that the human brain is powerfully affected when the body is exposed to bright light. Cooper also states many people report when they're exposed to bright sunlight, they experience a strong sense of calmness followed by a surge of energy. And even some extra indoor light, not much more than the intensity of a house lamp, can increase your energy level. With each ray of light, your eyes send neurological impulses and signals to your brain to say alert and energized.

Doctors also know that seasonal affective disorder, also called the winter blues, can be treated with exposure to sunlight or full spectrum lighting produced by light machines that mimic sunlight. Exposure to sunlight also enhances our immune system and facilitates our skin's production of Vitamin D leading to healthier teeth and bones, according to a number of research reports.

While the benefits of finding the light are clear, please remember to make your time in the sun brief. We not only receive the greatest benefits from brief sunlight exposure but we also know the health consequences associated with spending too much time in the sun. Therefore doctors recommend that to get the maximum benefits of sunlight without the risks and side effects we have several choices. The following action steps represent several ways you can find the light depending on your schedule.

 ACTION STEPS

1. Exercise in the morning and soak up some morning sunlight.

2. Stretch, breathe and meditate outside in the morning for 20 minutes.

3. Take a brief sun break during your lunch break.

4. Here are a few resources regarding the effects of too much exposure to sunlight:

≈ Talk to your doctor.

≈ WebMD, www.webmd.com.

≈ Andrew Weil, M.D., www.drweil.com.

≈ Christiane Nothrup, M.D., www.drnorthrup.com.

EMBRACE THE ENERGY
OF SILENCE

*When you're in solitary confinement and you're six feet under without light, sound
or running water, there is no place to go but inside. And when you
go inside, you discover that everything that exists in the
universe is also within you.*

RUBIN CARTER, THE HURRICANE

As I write this I am sitting in my office, looking out the window, and watching a beautiful sunrise. My house is quiet. The kids are asleep and the world is silent, if only for a brief moment. Yet it is these brief moments where the energy sits, waiting to be tapped, where ideas originate and out of nothing flows everything. The greatest of inventors will tell you that their revolutionary ideas came through after moments of silence, just as scientists say that before the big bang all that existed was silence. For all of us the energy of silence is essential to creating anything meaningful in our lives.

They say it's the spaces between the notes that make the music and the pauses between sentences that make the speech. Perhaps it can also be said that it's the silence in between the noise of the world that makes our life worth living. Without silence, spaces and pauses, our lives would be filled with endless noisy chatter. Sirens, cars, horns, construction, radios, television, and people all contribute to the constant noise that fills our ears and minds with a bombardment of stimuli. Many days the noise doesn't stop. Yet the energy of silence waits—for that brief moment when the door shuts and the noise stops. Underneath the noise of all things is the silence of everything. It waits patiently for us to close our eyes and sit down. It waits for us to take our deep breaths. Then, when our thoughts are silent and the world stops moving, the energy of silence can be felt. Within the silence, sits the energy to recharge our batteries—to refuel our tired lives—to help us create.

All we have to do is tap it.

If you're like most people, you know the energy of silence allows you to tune out noisy distractions and tune in our most powerful sources of energy. And with each embrace, you feel a deeper connection with yourself and your higher power—whichever name or religion you choose. Yet, as you read this, you're probably saying, "I don't embrace the energy of silence enough." Well, I urge you now to remember the energy you feel when you close your eyes, clear your breath, and free your mind of noises and thought and let this feeling inspire you to seek out more silent moments in our noisy world. Thankfully there are many convenient opportunities to incorporate silent moments into your work, school or parenting schedule. Here are a few.

 ACTION STEPS

1. When you are sitting at your computer, simply stop typing, close your eyes and imagine a beautiful sunset.

2. This one comes from Dr. Wayne Dyer. When driving use red lights as a time to take silent breaks. Close your eyes and free your mind. When the light turns green someone will surely let you know by honking their horn.

3. When you're folding the laundry, enjoy a few minutes of silence.

4. When you are sitting on the couch, turn off the television and embrace a moment of silence.

5. When you walk outside, take a break from your headphones and enjoy a few minutes of walking in silence.

RIDE THE ENERGY WAVE; DON'T FIGHT AGAINST THE CURRENT

When we take time to catch our breath and look around, a heartbeat can be found in the earth's deep constant rhythms...

ALEXANDRA CIPUZAK

I learned this technique a few years ago and it has made a world of difference. Human beings, like all things in nature, experience cycles. The earth rotates causing day and night. The tides go in, the tides go out. The seasons change and as energy beings our energy rises and falls many times within a 24-hour cycle.

In order to maximize your energy it is important to pay attention to your energy and notice when it is rising and falling. Do you feel a wave of energy coming on? Or is your energy meter at zero and everything you do is a struggle? Is the energy flowing or is it fighting? These observations help you use your energy cycles to your advantage. When you feel a surge of energy you can then ride the wave. Like a great surfer you can take that wave higher and farther performing incredible feats along the way. A sales person can make many of their calls during this time. A stay-at-home parent can do the house work of five people. A writer can write twice as much in the same amount of time.

In contrast when your energy is at a low point or crashing you don't want to fight against the current. If you have ever been in a river with the current flowing toward you, you know how much energy is used to swim against it. Instead of asking "Why am I so tired right now?" and drinking coffee or an artificial energy booster to fight your downturns and risking burnout, there is another way. During moments of low energy, you can go with the flow of the current. Take a short energy break. Go outside and get some fresh air. Drink a bottle of water. Five to 10 minutes will make the difference. This will help you recharge instead of draining more energy. Then when your energy surges again you can take full advantage.

When you ride your waves and flow with the current you will most likely notice what I noticed: that you are more productive and do not get burned out. Someone who constantly fights against the current with fake energy boosters may succeed in the short run but in the end their mind and body will wear down. Depriving yourself of sleep, breaks, and your body's biological needs will eventually take its toll. At some point sales will decline. House work will be left undone and writer's block will set in. In contrast a person who learns to flow with their energy will have more energy when they need it.

 ACTION STEPS

1. Pay attention to your energy levels throughout the day.

2. When you feel a surge of energy, ride the wave.

3. When you feel like your energy is crashing, take a short break.

GIVE YOURSELF AN ENERGY AUDIT

Where do you invest your energy? How much of it is spent with meaningful people in your life? How much is spent on work? What about distractions? How about bad habits? Or goals that really don't matter any more? Do you often relive events of the past?

I ask you to think about these questions because one of the most important things we can do to maximize our energy is to identify where we invest our energy. If 100 percent represents our total energy, then a piece of that 100 percent is invested in every person and group we spend time with. How much energy goes to people who help you become a better person?

Another piece of our energy is invested in our beliefs. Do you invest your energy in positive beliefs or negative beliefs? We also invest a portion of our energy in bad habits and good habits. Which do you engage in? Many of us unfortunately invest our energy in the past, in negative past events or people who have hurt us.

It is important to know where you invest your energy because the more energy you invest in negative beliefs, bad habits, distractions, and people who drain you, the less energy you have to invest in positive people, positive beliefs, and positive actions. If you invest a total of 70 percent on things that weaken you, this means you only invest 30 percent of your energy on building a better you. That's like spending only $30 out of every $100 to build a house and $70 out of every $100 to tear it down. Not very efficient or productive. With an investment like this it is very hard to build anything. Even worse the house will likely crumble. And we wonder why so many of us get sick and burnt out when we try to do too much. Our bodies shut down because it doesn't have enough energy to run properly.

Identifying where you invest your energy helps you begin the process of making better investments. I once had a very poor performing stock portfolio. The first step I took was to examine the stock portfolio, identify the bad investments, and discard them. Once you decide which negative investments you wish to discard, then you can begin to find better opportunities for your energy. Knowing that you are really only spending 30-40 percent of your energy on worthwhile investments will be a big eye opener for you and motivate you to invest your energy in what matters most. Just imagine what you could accomplish if you invested 70-100 percent in creating something positive.

 ACTION STEPS

1. List all of the people, groups, beliefs, habits and past people and events that receive a piece of your energy.

2. Now assign each investment a percentage out of 100 percent. If you add up all your investments the total should be 100 percent.

3. Then designate each investment as positive, negative, or neutral.

4. Add up your total percentage of positive investments.

5. Then add up your total percentage of negative investments.

6. Identify how much energy you are investing positively and negatively.

7. Read the next section to use your energy audit to take action.

INVEST YOUR ENERGY IN WHAT MATTERS MOST

Life begets energy. Energy creates energy. It is only by spending oneself wisely that one becomes rich in life.

ELEANOR ROOSEVELT

Once you decide where you are currently investing your energy, the next step is to decide what changes need to be made. What should be discarded and what in your life should receive more of your energy? A strategy I use during this process is to ask energy questions. Does this person increase my energy or zap my energy? Does a certain organization or business group increase my energy or drain my energy? Does it increase my business or simply take up my time? And the single most important question I ask is, am I investing my energy in what matters most? Does my continued investment in this person, group, belief, and habit make me a better person? Will it matter a year or two from now? Does it improve society and those closest to me? The answers will help you direct your energy where it should be spent.

When possible, the things in your life that drain your energy or don't really matter should receive a minute amount of your energy. Negative feelings about a person in the past should be let go so you can invest your energy to create your present and future. People who waste your time and energy should be replaced with those who enrich your life. Remember, for each of us, what matters most and what enriches us will be different. The key is to know what matters most to you and learn to invest a majority of your energy on these priorities.

When you invest your energy in what matters most you receive the biggest return on your investments. You use your energy to develop and create what you value most. Instead of knocking your building down you build it with one positive investment at a time. If you invest more time with your children you will see their growth immediately. If you invest in positive beliefs instead of negative thoughts you will create an annuity of positive events and people in your life. If you tune out distractions and spend more time where it matters most you will be more productive and successful in whatever you do. Investing your energy in what matters most will be the best investment you have ever made.

 ACTION STEPS

1. Decide what matters most. Make a list.

2. Decide what is keeping you from investing your energy in what matters most. Make a list.

3. Spend less time and energy on the things that are not important.

4. Spend more energy and time on the things that do matter most. Make appointments and add them to your calendar to help you incorporate them into your life.

5. Reevaluate often, as your priorities will most likely change throughout your life.

TAP THE ENERGY OF THOUGHT

We are Divine enough to ask and we are important enough to receive.

DR. WAYNE DYER

We often associate energy with physical aspects of every day life—oil, gas, electricity, and exercise. Yet our greatest natural resource for untapped potential energy often resides as the energy of thought. When we think, we send the energy of our thoughts out into the world and into our bodies. Did you ever wonder why so many people seem to have the same idea at once? You come up with an idea for an invention and a few months later you notice that someone else has invented it. Or how many times have you thought about a friend or relative and minutes later they call you? In every seminar I have ever given, every single person has had this happen to them more than once. Can all these experiences really be coincidences? They must occur because of the energy of thought. Just because we can't see the energy of thought doesn't mean it doesn't exist. Just because we can't fully explain it doesn't mean it isn't real. We also can't fully explain the way viruses work and we also can't see satellite signals or cell phone transmissions and yet their energies are being transmitted throughout our world every day.

Thoughts, like all energies, travel and attract other forms of energies. The earth attracts the moon. Our cells attract other cells. We are attracted to the energy of other people. Why should the energy of thought be any different? In addition to attracting other ideas, our positive thoughts have the power to attract people, money, jobs, opportunities, good fortune, and many other wonderful things into our lives. Like a magnet, our thoughts have the power to reach within ourselves and out to the world and attract the very things that we consciously think about.

In order to make the energy of your thoughts work for you, you have to stand up and tell yourself and the world what you want. A thought can't travel unless it is born first. To attract what you want, your thoughts must be created, believed, projected and received.

To create your thoughts you simply need to think about what you want in your life. What would you like to see happen? What is your dream? Who would you like to meet? How do you want to feel? Where would you like to live? Then you have to turn your wants into beliefs. It is not enough to want things to happen. You have to know that they are going to happen. In fact, you have to be even more convincing and believe that they have already happened. For example, if you want more money and wealth in your life, you should think and say to yourself, "I am wealthy. I accept all the wealth and money in my life," rather than thinking and saying, "I want money and wealth in my life." If you want to attract a new job and new opportunities you should say, "I have a new great job and I accept all the opportunities that are presented to me," rather than "I want a new job and I wish I had a new job."

At this point you might be asking, "How can I believe that something has happened if it hasn't happened yet?" This is a good question and the answer lies in the laws of energy and the way the world works.

Thoughts of "wanting" are weak energies. They are illusions: unreal objects and desires to you, the world and to other forms of energies. These weak energies are practically powerless and therefore exert no power. However, thoughts of belief and acceptance are powerful, concrete and real to you and the world. While you may not actually have that "something" in your life, the more you believe it *should* be in your life and *is* in your life, the more quickly and powerfully you will send out that positive, powerful energy. The world has no choice but to be attracted to you and bring you what you have already accepted. Because you believe, the energies of the world believe and belief then becomes reality.

Also realize that the more you believe and accept, the more the world believes and accepts. Thus, it is imperative that you project your beliefs to the world and that you project often. The more often you say and think positive affirmations, the more you convince yourself and the world that they are real. Affirmations help you replace negative thoughts with positive beliefs. The more you say them, the more you convince your subconscious to believe them. This creates a powerful magnetic energy that grows stronger with every affirmation. As a result you become more confident in yourself and in turn the world becomes more confident in you.

To help you get started affirming your life I have included examples of positive affirmations for different areas of your life. As you get comfortable with saying affirmations you will come up with your own style and favorites.

- ≈ I am <u>your name here</u>. I accept all the great things in my life.
- ≈ I am successful. I am happy. I am wealthy. I am healthy.
- ≈ I accept all the wealth in my life. I accept all the money that flows now through my life.
- ≈ I accept all the people and companies that want to work with me and my company.
- ≈ I accept a call today from_____. I accept the great things we will do together.
- ≈ Today I will accomplish_____. Today I make it happen. Now is the time. This is the place.
- ≈ I accept all the joy and happiness in my life. I accept all the special people in my life.
- ≈ I am healthy. My mind is healthy. My body is healthy.

ACTION STEPS

1. Write down five affirmations that are relevant to your life.

2. Focus on these affirmations. Visualize them happening in your mind. Believe that they are a part of your life. Without belief an affirmation is just empty words.

3. Say each affirmation with conviction several times a day.

4. If you experience a negative thought, replace it with a positive affirmation.

5. Pay attention and observe the positive results your affirmations have on your life.

6. Repeat these steps as you focus on different areas of your life.

PLAY TO WIN

Energy and persistence conquer all things.

BENJAMIN FRANKLIN

There was a time in most of our lives when we had no fear—that feeling when we jumped from the jungle gym and slammed our little bodies to the ground. Perhaps it was when we went on our first roller coaster, or when we were in high school or college and felt that there was nothing we couldn't do. No goal was unattainable. We were an unstoppable wave of energy that would think of something and then make it happen

Then, as time goes by, the world tells us more frequently that we can't do anything we want. In fact, the world gets more specific and says you can't do this and you can't do that. The doubters laugh at our goals and try to persuade us from going after our dreams. They say, "You're crazy. It's too hard. It's too much of a long shot. Why don't you do this instead? You should play it safe." They act as if dreams were meant for others but not people like us. They surround us with negative energy and try to instill their own fears and insecurities in us. We not only begin to know the word "fear," we start to understand what it's like to be fearful. With so many people telling us we can't do something and so few telling us we can, it's hard not to let fear into our lives.

Unfortunately this is how many of us go through life. The fear starts as a thought and the thought then become an emotion that affects our body and entire state of being. We have mortgages, rent, responsibilities, car payments, college payments, medical bills, and jobs. Many of us have even more responsibilities with families and children to support. The doubters point all of this out and inject their doubt and negativity in us. "You can't start your own business. What if it fails? How are you going to feed your children? You can't start a new career. You know how hard it is to make money acting. Why would you want to do that? You shouldn't go after a promotion. They'll never give it to you. You're too old to change careers and learn computers. Why would you want to do a silly thing like that?"

Whether you are 20 or 50, many of us become so scared of losing what we have that we don't go after what we truly want. We allow the negative energy of fear into our lives, which cuts off the flow of positive energy and paralyzes our desires. We play it safe and hold on so tight to the status quo that we never experience what could be. We believe the doubters and don't take chances that will move us one step towards our dreams. I call this "playing to lose." We see this in sports all the time when a team has the lead. They start to think about how not to lose instead of how to win. They hold on so tight to their lead that they start playing safe and scared. You can see it in their energy and body language. As a result the other team takes chances, plays with no fear and eventually gains the momentum and wins.

To live a life filled with positive energy we must learn to repel the negative energy of fear. Whether it comes from within or from another person we must eliminate fear from our life and replace it with a "play-to-win" mindset. While fear serves no purpose in your life, a play to win attitude will allow you to create anything you want. Playing to win requires a commitment to yourself that says even if you fail, you will never give up and never let your goals and dreams die. Those who play to win know that success is not given to us. It is pursued with all the energy and sweat we can muster. Obstacles and struggles are part of life and only serve to make us appreciate our success. If everything came easy we wouldn't know what it felt like to truly succeed. Obstacles are meant to be overcome. Fear is meant to be conquered. Success is meant to be achieved. They are all part of the game of life and the people who succeed play to win and never give up until the game is over.

I have seen this power first hand. Two years ago, I was working for a technology company, fearful of losing my job and going bankrupt. We had just moved, the company I worked for was in financial trouble and I had an expensive mortgage, two kids and no job prospects. One day I told my wife, "I'm not going to live like this. No fear anymore. I'm going to do what I was born to do." My plan was to open a restaurant so that it would provide us with the funds to pay our bills. Once it was successful I would have the foundation to begin my life's work of writing and speaking. Of course, part of me was scared but I knew I didn't have a choice. For me, living in fear was like dying. Sure enough, two years later, I have three successful restaurants and I am doing what I love—making a difference in other people's lives by sharing energy.

I stopped the fear from flowing through my life and I replaced it with an attitude that "I was going to make my dreams come true. Whatever it took, I would make it happen." Once I changed my attitude, positive energy started flowing into and out of my life and everything began falling in place. I thank God for all of the blessings I have received but I also know that it started with me deciding to play to win. If I can do it so can you.

ACTION STEPS

1. Identify the fear in your life. What makes you fearful?

2. Remind yourself that this fear serves no purpose. It only weakens you.

3. Use the power of appreciation. According to Dan Baker, Ph.D., coauthor of *What Happy People Know*, research shows that it is physiologically impossible to be

in a state of appreciation and a state of fear at the same time. So if you are feeling stressed or fearful, start thinking of things that you can appreciate. Who do you love? Who loves you? Do you have your health? What are you thankful for?

4. Decide to play to win. It's as easy as turning on a light switch.

ADAPT AND EVOLVE

You only live once—but if you work it right, once is enough.

JOE E. LEWIS

It seems that during the last two decades our society and lifestyle have been on fast forward. Computer chips get smarter and smaller every year. Technology does more for us every day. Soon our refrigerators will be able to order more milk from the grocery store and our air conditioners will email a repairman to come fix them. Just try to imagine a life without e-mail. It's almost impossible. Now we have wireless e-mail at our finger tips. I often like to say, the rules have changed and so have our lives.

The problem is that our society and technology are evolving faster than human beings can keep up. Our DNA and biological programming are ancient and the way we interact with the world is still very primitive. For example, our flight-or-fight impulses that ensured our survival now may cause us stress and harm when we feel threatened in an office environment. Or as human beings many of us now sit in a chair all day instead of being active. As I said earlier in the book, human beings were meant to chop wood, carry water, and work the land. Now, for many of us society dictates that we sit in an office with no view of nature and no physical activity. Our biological programming expects us to live and interact in a world that doesn't exist for many of us anymore. And we wonder why so many of us are depressed, overweight and tired. Only when we go on vacation do we experience a glimpse of what feels most natural. Of course, that's why so many of us are happy when we slow down our pace.

Well, since many of us have to work and can't take vacations every day, we have to develop another way. We also shouldn't have to become a beach bum in order to be happy. Since we can't change society because the pace of life will only continue to get faster, we have to change ourselves. We have to adapt and evolve to today's society. We can make minor adjustments to our daily schedule that will maximize our energy and rejuvenate ourselves. Like everything in nature, we must adapt to different conditions in order to survive. We must evolve and learn to use our energy efficiently and effectively to interact with a changing world. We can get back to the basics. Exercising, eating natural healthy food, sleeping, connecting with nature, and taking short breaks and pauses are just a few of the strategies that will help us adapt and evolve.

As you incorporate the various strategies presented in this book into your life you will find that instead of letting your environment control and drain you, you will control and energize your environment. You will skillfully and willfully address the challenges of today with information, knowledge, habits and techniques. They will become your tool set to change what needs to be changed and fix what needs to be fixed. You will adapt to today's society and become a stronger, more evolved, energized being.

👟 ACTION STEPS

1. To test your ability to adapt and evolve read the next section, "Make Technology Work for You" and try incorporating the action steps into your life for a week.

2. Observe whether these action steps make a difference in your energy and life.

MAKE TECHNOLOGY
WORK FOR YOU

Computers, mobile phones, wireless web phones, pagers, PDAs and every new gadget made with the latest technology are supposed to make our lives better. The marketers promote every new innovation as the product that will transform our lives, give us more time, make us more productive, and provide us with the freedom and power to go wherever and do whatever we want. In many ways, they are right. The potentials of new technologies are as great as the claims. However, in reality, the use, or I should say, misuse, of technology falls considerably short of the promises. In other words, we only use half of our brains when it comes to using new communication devices. We interrupt our meals with calls on our mobile phones. We see people talking on the mobile phone in a restaurant, instead of talking to the person across the table. We hear a person's entire conversation on the train as he talks into his earpiece. We check our e-mails about 20 times a day. On average, about five pagers and phones go off in the movie theater during the course of a two-hour movie. Communication devices that should give us more freedom actually become tracking devices so that anyone can find us anytime, anywhere—in the movies, in restaurants, in our homes, in the mall, and at the beach. In reality, we are always working because we can check our e-mail and voicemail from any computer, phone, or PDA and any client, employer, employee or co-worker can reach us on any device. In reality technology makes life more complicated rather than making it easier.

Don't blame technology. It is our fault because we allow technology to rule our lives instead of making technology work for us. I say this not as someone who sits on his high horse, but as someone who has become a sinner in the eyes of the technology gods. They often yell at me that I am giving their innovations a bad name. We need to stop being a slave to our phone and computer and other gadgets and become a master of our technology-filled world.

If you want to create a successful and energized life, you need to get rid of as many distractions as possible. This doesn't mean you need to get rid of technology. Rather you need to make technology work for you. Here are some ideas that have worked for me and other people who have shared their stories with me. Consider them Action Steps to help you maximize your energy.

 ACTION STEPS

1. Shut your phone off. It's as easy as pressing the power button when you don't want to be disturbed.

2. Ignore the call waiting feature. Focus on the person you are talking to and you'll feel better too.

3. Check your e-mail three times a day. This will help you be more productive and focus on what you have to do instead of checking every five minutes to see if someone emailed you.

LIVE 365 LIVES A YEAR FOR THE REST OF YOUR LIFE

I believe I understand life and death. And I am scared of neither.

IVAN GOLDFARB

As I mentioned earlier in the book, my parents divorced when I was a year old. Thankfully my mother married a wonderful person who raised me as his son. My dad was a tough New York City police officer who had hundreds of stories of near misses and close calls. Yet, one particular story has stood out in my mind over the years.

My dad and his partner chased a criminal into an abandoned building. As my dad searched, he moved quietly. The criminal came out of nowhere and placed a gun against my dad's head. My dad's heart began to race, fearing the worst. The criminal then pulled the trigger of the gun. It misfired. I repeat, the loaded gun misfired. My dad's partner was then able to knock down the criminal and they apprehended him. Through this story, my dad taught me that life can change in a moment. After that day my dad felt he was given a new lease on life. He should have been dead and yet he was alive because a gun misfired. It wasn't his time to go and thankfully my mom never had to receive the call she always feared would wake her up in the middle of the night. She never had to hear the words "Your husband was shot."

The truth is we never know when our time is up. Life is a gift and at any moment that gift can be taken away. We can let this reality put us in fear or help us make the most out of every day. The way I see it, if cats have nine lives then we need to live like we have 365 lives per year for the rest of our lives. In essence, this means that we should begin a new "life" every day. We need to wake up each morning and celebrate that we have been given another life to live and make the most of that life. We also need to think about how we would live if we knew that at the end of the day there would be no tomorrow. We don't do this to bring ourselves down but to remind ourselves of the precious gifts of health and life. You need to ask yourself, "If I die tomorrow, would I be happy with the way I lived my life? Would I be proud of my accomplishments? What would my epitaph say? Would I have taken more chances? Did I live my life to the fullest? Did I make a difference in other people's lives? Did I smile enough?"

Your answers will help you focus your life and concentrate on living each day to the max—maximum energy and maximum joy. If you're not satisfied with your answers, the good news is that there is still today and there is still time to make today count. While a play to win attitude helps us live a life without fear, living 365 lives a year helps us make the most of every day. We can live with boundless energy and enthusiasm for today and only today. We don't have to imprison ourselves in our unfulfilled dreams and unrealized potential. We can go for it. We can pursue our dreams and live the life we have always wanted. We can be free to succeed. Failure? Why should we care about failure if we are creating our life every day? At the end of the day failure is dead. Tomorrow begins a new day, a new life, and a new opportunity to succeed.

ACTION STEPS

1. Wake up each morning and say, "Today I begin my new life."

2. Live 365 lives a year for the rest of your life.

3. Ask yourself often, "Am I making the most of today or am I living for tomorrow?" This will help you be conscious of your choices and actions.

HAVE A
"BIG BANG" MINDSET

Power is the faculty or capacity to act, the strength and potency to accomplish something. It is the vital energy to make choices and decisions. It also includes the capacity to overcome deeply embedded habits and to cultivate higher, more effective ones.

STEVEN R. COVEY

Life is a choice. And every day you can choose to have a big bang mindset. You can choose to believe that you create your life every day through your words, thoughts, choices and actions. While we have all been created, we now have the opportunity to create our lives one thought, one word, one choice, one action, one energy source at a time.

Where Richard Carlson tells us not to sweat the small stuff, and he's right, I believe that life is all about the little things. We don't create our lives by focusing on the big things. The big projects, the big promotion, the big car, the big house. Rather we create our life by doing the little things and allowing the big things to happen. If we read one book a week for 30 years, that equals 1,560 books. That's a lot of knowledge. If we put basil in a burrito instead of cilantro the taste would change dramatically. The difference between rain and snow is only a few degrees. They say football is a game of inches. To reduce crime in New York City, former Mayor Rudy Guilianni focused on preventing small crimes. What he and the world found out was when you arrest people for small crimes you get big reductions in murders and other felonies. As someone who has owned restaurants, I have found that a restaurant's success is all about the little things. Success is built one customer, one meal, one ingredient at a time. Our lives are no different.

When we have a big bang mindset we accept responsibility for our life. We know that we have the power to create success or succumb to failure. Our life is the result of each choice we make and each action we take. A positive thought leads to a new opportunity in your life. A positive conversation with a group of people leads to a plethora of new friends and contacts. Walking in the morning before work makes you feel more energized which leads to a promotion. Choosing fruit, nuts and raisins as snacks instead of snickers bars and chips on a daily basis makes a big difference in your health and energy level. Drinking green tea instead of coffee in the afternoon day after day will increase your energy over time and help protect you against cancer.

It's not the big things that you do once that matter. It's the little things that you do every minute of every day that means everything. With a big bang mindset you realize that life is a series of seconds and moments that when added together equals your life. You are a work in progress, a creation that is still being created. Therefore, with a big bang mindset you seize each moment to create the life you want. You create your life one thought, one word, one choice, one action at a time.

 ACTION STEPS

1. Focus on your thoughts. Are you choosing positive thoughts or negative thoughts?

2. Focus on your words. Are you surrounding yourself with positive words or negative words? Are you speaking positively about life or are you always complaining?

3. Focus on your choices. Are you making good choices that benefit you or bad choices that hurt you?

4. Focus on your actions. What are you doing to create your life? Do you have a good plan and not follow through or do you take action on your positive thoughts and plans.

SOUP UP YOUR LIFE

Growing up in a Jewish-Italian family, chicken soup was a big part of my child. As soon as one of us became sick with a cold or fever, Mom made a pot of chicken soup and we always felt better. Well, now we know that chicken soup does more than nourish the body and soul. Researchers at Johns Hopkins University in Baltimore discovered that chicken soup and other soups increase our energy while also reducing fat cravings. The research showed that people ate significantly less during their meals if they had soup beforehand. Furthermore, out of many different appetizers soup was considered the most satisfying and invigorating. Note that not all soups are created equally. We should avoid beef-base, pork-base, and cream-base soups when it comes to eating food for energy.

While this kind of scientific research is helpful, we also know from our personal experience that a healthy soup gives us energy. As a child, I remember coming into the house after playing football and eating a bowl of soup. It always rejuvenated me. Or today, before I wrote this, I had soup and a salad for lunch. Afterwards I felt completely energized. How does soup make you feel? After a hearty and healthy bowl do you feel energized? If so, try to eat soup more often for more energy. To help you soup up your life here are a few ways to eat more soup.

 ACTION STEPS

1. Visit your local health food store or the health food section of your super market and notice the different brands

and types of soup. Read the ingredients and you will notice they are made with natural ingredients and often less sodium.

2. Buy a few of the soups that you like.

3. If you work in an office, bring your soup in a container or bowl and eat it as a snack to keep you going until lunch or eat it during lunch with a salad or sandwich, or as an appetizer.

4. Eat soup before dinner as an appetizer and eat a light energizing dinner.

5. Once a week make a different kind of soup and keep it available in the refrigerator. You might make a vegetable soup one week, lentil soup the next, and chicken soup after that. When you get hungry soup it up.

6. Check out various soup books such as: "Saved by Soup: More Than 100 Delicious Low-Fat Soup Recipes to Eat and Enjoy Every Day" by Judith Barrett.

7. Visit www.souprecipe.com for hundreds of great soup recipes.

TONE YOUR TUMMY

According to researchers, your abdominal muscles are a key source of strength and energy. Strong abdominal muscles help you maintain better posture which helps you breathe better and inhale more energizing oxygen into your lungs. This means more energy for your brain and body. While stomach exercises are most everyone's least favorite exercise they are essential to a strong abdominal region and increased energy.

While there are many forms of stomach exercises, I have found the stomach crunch to be most effective for me. Stomach crunches, when done properly, allow you to focus on building your stomach muscles without hurting your back. Stomach exercises should include slow and steady movements in order to maximize the tension placed on the stomach muscles. Avoid fast, uncontrolled movements that may cause you harm. As with any exercise I recommend you consult an exercise book such as *Body for Life*, a magazine such as *Shape* or a personal physical trainer. One session with a physical trainer should be enough to teach you the basics. Here are a few tips to help you tone your tummy.

🥾 ACTION STEPS

1. Do your stomach exercises in the morning when you get out of bed. All it takes is a few minutes each morning to increase your energy for a lifetime.

2. At first this habit will take getting used to but soon it

will become a natural part of your routine.

3. If the morning isn't a good time for abdominal exercises then when you get home from work, change into comfortable clothes and do your exercises then.

LET YOUR ENERGY SHINE

Our deepest fear is not that we are inadequate. Our deepest fear is that we are powerful beyond measure. It is our light, not our darkness that frightens us. We ask ourselves, who am I to be brilliant, gorgeous, talented, and fabulous? Actually, who are you not to be? You are a child of God.

MARRIANNE WILLIAMSON

In a world of infinite possibilities, choices and combinations, there has never been, nor will there ever be, anyone like you. You are an original—one of a kind. You may breathe like everyone and talk like most, but your fingerprints are unmatched and your eye's retina is distinct. You are an energy being like everyone and yet everyone is not like you.

Many of us may wear khaki pants, yet each one of us is unique. Underneath the hood, you are the only model exactly like you that will ever exist. Is this scary? I don't think so. I think it's fascinating. What I think is scary is that many of us don't let our uniqueness show. We don't live the lives we were born to live. We don't tap that unique power source inside us. Each one of us is born with a purpose. Each one of us has a unique source of energy to give to the world. It is a gift. When that gift is given to the world we see presents everywhere. Michael Jordan playing basketball, Mozart composing music, Nicole Kidman and Jodie Foster acting, Michelangelo painting, Mia Hamm playing soccer and Caroline Myss giving a lecture about energy. The list goes on.

We also see these gifts in everyday life. A singing waiter who is always happy. A doorman who makes everyone's day every day. A mom who can feed her kids, talk on the phone with the doctor, make lunch for tomorrow, do the laundry, sing the alphabet and still loves every minute. A clothing designer who dreams of new designs and fabrics. A writer who feels that writing is like breathing. Each of these people and millions more, doing what they do best. Tapping into their unique skill set and making a difference. Doing what they were born to do and shining light onto the world.

But what about the millions of people who don't let their energy shine? Their gifts are still undiscovered in the depths of miserable jobs and unhappy lives. Their light clouded by the darkness of resentment. Hidden by the desire to fit in and be like everyone else. Masked by settling for a paycheck and the status quo. Covered by fear of shining too bright, as Marianne Williamson suggests.

How about you? Do you let your energy shine? Or are your gifts still hidden to yourself and the world? Do you know what makes you unique and different? This is the best place to start. Ask yourself "Who do I admire and what do they do? What do I enjoy doing? What are my skills?" Decide what you would do if money was no object. Where would you devote your time? If you had one day left on earth what gift would you give the world before you die? Perhaps it's your love and this is your purpose. Not everyone is born to paint, sing, or act. Perhaps your purpose is to raise wonderful children who will shine the brightest of lights onto the world. Spend time doing things for yourself. Have fun and do things you like to do. When we enjoy life, our purpose often finds us.

No matter what your gift is I believe it is important to discover it and believe in it. Once it is found it is essential to open it. Once it is opened it is imperative that you let it shine and light up the world. When you let your energy shine, you unleash an awesome amount of energy that fuels your life and the lives of many others. So let your energy shine and light up the world.

ACTION STEPS

1. Identify what makes you unique and different. Perhaps

everyone says that you are one of the friendliest persons they have ever met.

2. Identify what you are good at. What are you great at? What are your skills?

3. Identify what you love to do. What brings you joy? Satisfaction? What jobs do you seem attracted to? Who do you admire and what do they do?

4. Take care of yourself. Do things that you enjoy. Let your purpose find you.

5. Spend the time to cultivate these gifts and share them with others. During the day at work, or in a new career, or after work, or on weekends, decide on one action you will take to let your energy shine. My friend Amy chose to be a comedian at night while working as a pharmaceutical rep during the day. Now she thrives doing both and is living her dream.

6. Let your energy shine.

7. Read *What Should I Do With My Life* by Po Bronson and/or *The Pathfinder: How to Choose or Change Your Career for a Lifetime of Satisfaction and Success* by Nicholas Lore.

DRINK GREEN TEA

I am a big fan of Green Tea. I promote its benefits whenever I speak and love hearing from all the people who share with me how Green Tea has improved their health and enhanced their energy. I first learned about the benefits of Green Tea from my favorite health and wellness expert, Dr. Andrew Weil, author of *Eight Weeks to Optimum Health*. The Chinese have been drinking green tea for years and now numerous studies are reporting that green tea helps us fight against cancer and prevent heart disease.

While all "real" tea comes from the same plant Camellia sinensis, the benefits of green tea result because of the way the leaves are processed. According to Dr. Weil, instead of crushing the leaves, piling them in heaps and briefly "sweating" them for black tea, for green tea, the tea leaves are steamed, rolled and dried, a method that preserves the content of polyphenols, anti-oxidant compounds that give us health benefits. Dr. Weil states these anti-oxidants protect our heart by lowering cholesterol and improving lipid metabolism and guard against cancer by scavenging for free radicals that can damage cells and push them in the direction of uncontrolled growth. They also have antibacterial effects.

But there is more to the Green Tea story. In addition to the health benefits of green tea, I drink it and recommend it because it is a great alternative to coffee and caffeinated energy drinks. Green Tea contains anywhere from 26 mg to 40 mg of caffeine, about half or one-third the amount of coffee. Like coffee, it gives you an energy boost to kick start your day or wake you up in the afternoon. Yet because it doesn't contain as much caffeine, green tea doesn't take you as high as coffee and doesn't cause you to crash as well. Where coffee may cause you to have the caffeine jitters, green tea doesn't stimulate your body as much. I have found that Green Tea gives me more of a sustained source of energy. Rather than soaring and crashing, I feel a steadier rise in my energy level and never really notice when it gradually falls. The effects of Green Tea feel more like an energy boost than an energy jolt.

Many of the people who have switched to Green Tea after taking my seminar have reported that they feel more clear headed in the afternoon after drinking Green Tea instead of coffee or other caffeinated drinks. And most importantly they don't feel like they are being taken on an energy roller coaster ride. The great thing about green tea is that now you can buy it almost anywhere. So buy a box and test it for yourself. If it works for you, like it does for me, Green Tea will become another great source of energy for your life.

ACTION STEPS

1. Try drinking a cup of Green Tea in the morning. You can drink it hot. Or you can drink it cold by letting it cool down in your refrigerator or pouring it over ice.

2. Drink Green Tea instead of coffee, caffeinated sodas and energy drinks.

3. If you are a big fan of your morning coffee like my wife then have your coffee in the morning but replace your afternoon cup of coffee with a cup of Green Tea.

Note: If you must stay away from caffeine for medical reasons, de-caffeinated Green Tea is also available and provides your body with anti-oxidants as well. When choosing a de-caffeinated Green Tea, select a brand that is naturally de-caffeinated without chemicals.

TRASH THE HYDROGENATED OILS

If you read the ingredients on most of the products found in supermarkets you will see the words, "partially hydrogenated" or "hydrogenated oil." Hydrogenated oil is found in almost everything from margarine, shortening (i.e., Crisco), breads, crackers, cookies, soups, sauces, frozen meals, desserts and chips. Unfortunately for us, according to many health experts, putting hydrogenated oils into your body is like putting tar into your veins or sludge into a car's engine.

Through the hydrogenation process, hydrogen is pumped into liquid unsaturated oil in order to solidify it and give it a longer shelf life. This process of heating oil to solidify it produces trans fatty acids (TFAs) which are very harmful to our bodies. Clinical studies have shown that trans-fat raises LDL cholesterol levels, the bad cholesterol, while lowering the HDL levels, the good cholesterol in your body—increasing your risk of coronary heart disease. According to Dr. Weil, although we know the body uses natural fatty acids to construct cell membranes and hormones, we don't know how it handles TFAs. He says there is reason to believe these fats cause derangements of cell structure, thus promoting cancer. He also predicts we will soon be hearing a lot more about their hazards.

Increasing awareness about the health hazards of TFAs and hydrogenated oils are even causing major food companies to make changes. In fact, Frito-Lay now offers trans fat-free Doritos, Cheetos and Tostitos. They use expeller pressed oil as opposed to partly hydrogenated soybean oil. When these healthier products first hit the shelves I was spotted dancing in the aisle of my local grocery store. And McDonald's announced that they would change their frying oil to reduce its trans-fat content. While this is good news and I hope someone reading this book five years from now will laugh at the fact that hydrogenated oil was even once an ingredient in many of our processed foods, there is no guarantee this will happen. Therefore until large food manufacturers make their changes we have to make our changes.

If you think of your body as an energy machine, then consider hydrogenated oils as the sludge that will decrease the performance of your engine. Your engine is made up of 100 trillion energy cells and when you fuel them with bad oil, you get less output and have less energy. When you feed your cells good oils, such as olive oil, you ensure peak performance. It's as simple as bad oils equals bad energy. Great oils equals great energy. Dr. Weil believes that TFAs are so bad for us he recommends that we eliminate them from our diet as much as possible. Here are a few ways to trash the hydrogenated oils.

 ACTION STEPS

1. Remember one of my favorite sayings from Dr. Weil. Manufacturers hydrogenate oil to give products a longer shelf life. However, a longer shelf life for them means a shorter shelf life for you.

2. Check the labels and ingredients of any processed foods you buy and avoid those containing hydrogenated or partially hydrogenated oils of any kind.

3. Buy snacks, breads, crackers, soups and many other products from your local health food store, the health food section of your supermarket or from a store such as Whole Foods. Many of these stores will have products that contain expeller- pressed organic oils instead of hydrogenated oils.

4. Avoid fast food restaurants unless you know they use healthy oils.

PRACTICE THE 90-10 RULE

I was having desert in a restaurant once with my wife when a person who attended one of my seminars came up to me and said, "Hey, you're the energy guy. You can't be eating dessert." It was a funny moment; we all laughed, and I had to explain my 90-10 rule which she did not remember hearing at my seminar. I want to share my 90-10 rule with you to both help you make long lasting changes in your life and create an understanding between us just in case we happen to see each other eating dessert in a restaurant. We'll nod at each other, smile and know the 90-10 rule is in effect.

The two fundamental principles of the 90-10 rule are: 1) We should eat healthy, energizing, natural food 90 percent of the time; and 2) we all deserve to treat ourselves. I am a firm believer that if we deprive ourselves of our favorite treats such as ice cream, deserts, donuts, candy then our lives as Energy Addicts will never feel natural or sustained. It's like a diet that says you can only eat meat or an exercise program that says you have to work out in a gym five days a week. At some point it will be difficult to maintain these programs and diets because they don't flow with our natural lifestyles and rhythms. They feel forced and once we stop them we revert back to our old habits. I believe the best programs and the best diets help people incorporate lifelong habits into their lives. Instead of a diet or program, these habits become who we are. They become our way of life.

The 90-10 rule says that instead of eating deserts, candy, unhealthy and energy draining foods a majority of the time, like many Americans do, we should eat energizing foods 90% of the time and enjoy our treats, candy, and deserts once in a while. You can be an Energy Addict without depriving your-self. This helps your short-term changes become lifelong habits. Going out on a date night with your significant other? Enjoy desert after dinner. Taking your kids to the amusement park? Eat some cotton candy and ice cream. You can do this and not feel guilty because you eat great sources of energy most of the time. You don't eat donuts, Pop Tarts, cookies and candy every day so when its time to enjoy a treat, you enjoy a treat without any hesitation or fear of consequence. You know you fuel your body with the best fuel 90 percent of the time and 10 percent of the time you treat yourself and satisfy your cravings. Otherwise you will always feel like your miss-ing something. Always in want of a treat? In many cases that treat will have power over you. By not depriving yourself you eliminate any unbalanced neediness and you put treats right in their place. You put them right where they belong—in your stomach only 10 percent of the time.

 ACTION STEPS

1. When you first start eating healthier energizing foods plan a treat three times a week. Once on Monday, once on Wednesday and once on Friday. You are in the habit form-ing stage at this point and thus structure is important.

2. After a month scale back your treats to 2 times a week.

3. After you feel like eating healthy energizing meals and snacks has truly become a comfortable habit then you should eat treats 10 percent of the time whenever the sit-uation or desire presents itself.

4. I am confident that after eating energizing food 90 per-cent of the time you will actually not want to eat treats that much because they will make you tired. Once you eat them you will feel their negative effects immediately.

ENERGIZE WITH YOGA

What lies before us and what lies behind us is nothing compared to what lies within us.

RALPH WALDO EMERSON

Celebrities such as Madonna have recently helped popularize yoga in America. Hatha yoga, the most familiar form of yoga practiced in this country, is but one small branch of a rich history of yogic tradition. No one can exactly pinpoint when yoga was born, but historical evidence is apparent from over five thousand years ago. A fully integrated spiritual path called yoga came into existence between two and three thousand years ago.

The word "yoga" is a Sanskrit term that means "union" or "joining." Teachers explain yoga is the joining or uniting of the mind, body and spirit to improve our life, and enhance our health. Ultimately, yoga breaks down inner barriers that create pain and suffering and reunite the practitioner with the true self. As business Yogi Megan McDonough says, "We're so used to seeing ourselves as limited labels—mother, father, executive, teacher—that we can miss the pervasive vastness of our own nature. Our true nature is limitless."

Hatha means "force," and it is the branch of yoga that is based on physical postures called asanas—of which there are thousands—and breath controls called pranayama. From this point of physical purification, hatha yoga helps a person connect with inner energy, quiets a busy mind, and increases physical, mental and spiritual energy. The physical and mental aspects of yoga help your mind and body become one. The spiritual aspects help you become one with the energy of everything. With each pose and breath you connect with your own energy and the energy of the universe. Yoga helps you increase your flexibility and tones your muscles. I used to have neck problems and pinched nerves until I started yoga and now I am pain free.

Yoga also includes breathing exercises that help you focus your mind and body on the present moment. With each breath you fill your body with energy and unite the energy outside you with the energy inside you. This union allows you to feel like one whole energy being rather than someone who's energy is being scattered in different directions. With yoga, everything is right here, right now. With each breath, each movement, and each moment of silence you unite and energize your mind, body and spirit. And one of the best things about yoga is that you don't need equipment or a special room. All you need is you and a small area of space. With yoga you can energize your life anytime, anywhere.

 ACTION STEPS

1. Visit www.yogajournal.com for postures, techniques and information, or www.yoga.com for articles and books, and www.yrec.org for the philosophical underpinnings of yoga.

2. Visit www.gaiam.com or www.amazon.com to shop for yoga videos and yoga products. Or go to your local library and check out the video for a few weeks. I got started when my wife introduced me to Rodney Yee's "Yoga for Beginners."

3. Follow a yoga video as part of your morning routine.

4. Do yoga as a family a little while after dinner. Make it fun.

5. Introduce your kids to yoga. The natural animal-like

poses are very easy for kids to follow. My three-year-old son loves doing the cobra and cat poses.

6. Have a yoga themed party. A new trend is taking place where instructors will come to your home and teach yoga poses at a party. Forget twister. It's time for Yoga. This also works for kids' parties especially since animals are so popular among children and yoga involves animal poses.

7. If you work for a corporation my favorite yoga teacher, speaker and trainer is Megan McDonough. Visit her at www.urinfinityinabox.com. As a business yogi she helps people work with ease using introspective yoga techniques.

BECOME A
WALKING TOURIST

This strategy is one of my favorite ways to energize my life. When I go on vacation or visit another city on business I become a walking tourist. Whenever I have the chance I walk around the city and take in all of the energy it has to offer. I see the sights; listen to the noises on the street; hear the conversations outside the corner stores; watch people hustle and bustle about their day.

Once when I was in San Diego I walked about five miles from my hotel to the Coronado Bridge. The sights were breathtaking and the energy was peaceful. As a native New Yorker I have been to New York City many times and have been known to walk ten to 15 miles in a given day. Instead of taking the time to wave down a taxi, I just keep on walking. On my walks I literally feed off the energy of the city. I look at the different buildings; watch people selling different merchandise on the streets; inhale the aromas from fine restaurants and delight in the smell of roasted nuts and hot pretzels. I love listening to all of the sounds of the people, places and machines that create the energy of a thriving city. Before I know it I have walked for two hours and I'm ready for more. Whatever city I am walking, I simply take in all it has to offer.

From New York to Miami and San Francisco to San Diego I not only walk the city with my legs, I see it with my eyes and hear it with my ears. With each sight I see and each conversation I hear, I engage all of my senses. With each step I take and each person I meet I energize my body and my mind. Becoming a walking tourist is easy. All you have to do is take a walk and take in the energy around you. So when you're visiting a city for the first time, sure, take the city bus tours they offer. Then become a walking tourist and see the city another way.

 ACTION STEPS

1. When you are on vacation or business, carve out time in your day to walk around the town or city you are visiting.

2. Instead of exercising in a hotel gym, weather permitting, consider walking around the city or town for your morning or evening exercise.

3. Instead of relying on taxi-cabs to travel short distances, consider walking a few miles.

BECOME A WALKING TOURIST IN YOUR HOME TOWN

While it's great to be a walking tourist in a new city, it's also possible to become a walking tourist in your home town or city. Sometimes it's more fun to see what's new in your familiar world. I live in a beach community and I always consider myself a walking tourist. I take long walks and I look at everything around me to see what's new. I notice that certain houses have added new flowers. One house has been painted; another house is getting a new driveway. Sometimes kids are playing in the street. Other times a dog I have not seen before barks at me. Many times I'll see the same faces pass me and some days I'll pass a new face. I wonder if they are visiting or perhaps they just moved to the area. I also breathe in the fresh air and the smell is always different. I look at the trees and listen to the birds sing and watch the squirrels play. You can actually take the same walk every day and always see something different. Try and see for yourself.

Something new is always happening. We just have to look for it. A walking tourist doesn't walk with their head down staring at their feet. They look at anything and experience everything. A walking tourist with an eye out for something new will never be disappointed. There are clouds to paint in the sky and songs to sing with the birds. A walking tourist is never in want of new energy. They experience it every day. They feel it, see it, hear it and live it.

So if you are ever feeling tired or in need of some energy, simply take a walk and engage your senses. Fuel your life with new sights, sounds, smells and experiences at home or away from home. For a walking tourist everything is different but the results are the same. More fuel for the mind and more energy for the body.

 ACTION STEPS

1. Take frequent walks around your city or town.

2. Look for things that have changed or are changing.

3. Look, listen, and smell while you walk. Engage your senses.

4. Walk with the feeling that you are going to experience something new. When you have this feeling amazing things will happen.

TAP INTO THE ENERGY OF NOW

Love the moment and the energy of that moment will spread beyond all boundaries.

CORITA KENT

Spiritual teacher Eckhart Tolle, author of one of my favorite books, *The Power of Now* teaches that people are happiest when they live in the "now." He explains that only when we free ourselves from our mind and constant thoughts are we able to experience the power of the present moment. He teaches that our energy is greatest in the "now." When we constantly think about the past or the future our energy is both here and there. By thinking of another time and living now, we are essentially splitting our energy and weakening it with each past or future thought. We might be eating lunch but we are steaming about the argument we had with our colleague in the morning. Or perhaps we are playing with our kids but thinking about how it will be more fun when they are older. Our bodies may be here but our minds are always somewhere else. However, when we tap into the power of now, we allow all of our energy to be in one place. Now. Not in the future or in the past, but now.

When we tap into the energy of now we find tremendous power, peace and happiness. I don't say this as a teacher who is there yet, but as someone who is still learning. I believe we teach what we need to learn and each day I learn to be present and tap into the energy of now. I have found the more often I live in the now, the more energy I have. Living in the past and future can be very draining. With each past and future thought we essentially invest our energy into a vacuum. Energy spent in the past or future is worthless now. It's like investing money in a company that already went bank-rupt or hasn't even been created yet. We can't do anything with energy spent in the past or the future. It just gets wasted.

In contrast, when we tap into the energy of now we cre-ate an abundance of energy. Food tastes better if we eat in the now. Work is more rewarding if we work moment to moment. And life is more enjoyable if we live for today and not for tomorrow. In the now we don't need anything nor do we want anything. We already have it right now. We are happy now. We are satisfied now. We are thankful now. We are successful now. We are focused now. Everything that we will ever create in our lives will always be created in the now. In the future anything is possible, but in the now the possible happens.

Ironically, the more we live in the now the more the things we used to desire will find us. Instead of searching, we will be found. This happens because we become a more pow-erful magnet of energy when we focus all of our energy now. Instead of scattering our energy it grows stronger within us. Other forms of energy such as money, people, and opportu-nities are attracted to our energy field in much the same manner in which the earth is attracted to the sun.

They say that being present is truly a present that only you can give yourself. So give yourself a gift by tapping into the energy of now. Become skilled at living in the now and watch as you transform your life from wanting to having. The now is not always an easy place to find, especially in today's hurried culture. However, if you think of each day as a series of moments, start by trying to be present in each moment and practice often. When you are talking to your friend, don't think of what you are going to make for dinner. Only talk to your friend. When you are playing with your kids, watch their expressions. Feel their love. Get into the kid zone. In each moment exists an opportunity to tap into the power of now. When you do this with increasing frequency a tremendous amount of energy will be created and amazing things will happen in your life.

DON'T BE A WAITER

I never think of the future. It comes soon enough.

ALBERT EINSTEIN

I believe everyone should wait tables once in their life so they can learn to appreciate the people who make their living off of the tips and generosity of others. Wait tables once and you will have a new appreciation for the difficulty of this job. I waited tables after college and the experience was invaluable. It taught me customer service, presentation skills and people skills.

While everyone should try being a waiter of tables, I also believe no one should be a waiter of life. A waiter of life is someone who always waits for everything to happen. Instead of living now and tapping the energy of now, they wait for the future and put their energy into the future. A waiter is always thinking of their next accomplishment, and next vacation. They wait for tomorrow to be happy. They wait for a bigger house, a bigger car, and a bigger paycheck to be satisfied. When tomorrow comes, they are still not content. Then they can't wait to buy a second house and a second car. A waiter so badly wants the future to be now they get very anxious when they are in traffic or a line at the grocery store. Ironically, a waiter of life doesn't wait very well at all. They bang their steering wheel in traffic, make faces at the grocery clerk, and fidget as they wait for an appointment or meeting. A waiter is always thinking of tomorrow so they never enjoy today.

I still find myself being a waiter at times but much less than I used to. In the past I was the busiest waiter I knew. I was always thinking of the future. I would project my life into the future and imagine how happy I would be. But I was never happy now. I would often say, "I can't wait until the kids are older. Then we'll have fun." Or I would think when I save a certain amount of money in the bank I'll be happy. My wife, who is a great teacher, would often respond, "What about now? If you're not happy now, you'll never be happy." Everything changed when I made a conscious decision to give up my job as a waiter of life. I practiced not waiting and like everything in life, if we practice we will get better.

We can all practice not being a waiter. Try it in everyday situations. Next time you are in traffic don't think about the fact you might be late. Just close your eyes and take a deep breath and relax. Focus on how you feel right now. Or if you are waiting in a line at the supermarket, don't let yourself get frustrated. Enjoy the time you have standing there. Think about what you are thankful for. Thank God you are able to stand in a line.

And when it comes to goals and hopes for the future, apply the Buddhist teaching of non-attachment and detach from your goals. This didn't mean you give them up. Goals serve a great purpose. It means that you decide to focus on the present and not attach yourself to any future outcome or event. You realize it's not about the future car, house or job. If you achieve your goal, great; however, your happiness is not tied to your goal. You don't live for the goal. You live for the present. The goal is where you want to go but now is where you are. Like driving to a family gathering in another state, you need to know where you are going in order to get there. However, the only way you get there is by driving one mile at a time. If you lose sight of the road you might crash and the future will never become the present.

When you give up your job as a waiter you will create more energy in your life. Like we discussed in the energy of now, instead of your energy being split, it will all be here and now. This will allow you to focus on today and now, instead of thinking about tomorrow and the future. This means more energy for our lives and less energy for our future, imagined life. Ironically, when we stop being a waiter the future is better than we could have imagined.

 ACTION STEPS

1. Use your time standing in lines to practice not being a waiter.

2. If you often sit in traffic practice enjoying the time in your car.

3. If you find yourself thinking you will happier in the future, work on being happier now.

4. Read or listen to the book *The Power of Now*.

SWITCH YOUR CANDY BOWL WITH A FRUIT BOWL

This simple change has improved the energy of virtually everyone I know who has tried it. One of the main issues here is convenience. If you walk into your office or home and there is a bowl of candy on the desk or counter it is very easy to grab it. Why not? After all, it's sitting right there, calling our names. I used to work in an office where candy and chocolate sat on just about everyone's desk. When someone became hungry they grabbed some chocolate or candy. Does this sound like your office? By having a candy bowl so easily available it literally takes a tremendous amount of energy and willpower not to eat it on a regular basis. The same goes for our homes. If we keep a candy bowl on the kitchen counter, sure enough we'll grab for it every time. Hunger sets in, and we reach for the candy.

Thankfully there is a simple solution to this problem. Make the switch.

Replace your candy bowl in your office or home. You'll not only increase your energy but you'll energize your co-workers or family members. By making fruit easily and conveniently available, perhaps they will ask you to have a piece of fruit. At first they may say, "Hey wait a minute. What happened to the candy?" This will provide a great opportunity to explain to your co-workers how a piece of fruit in the afternoon will help them not to crash like usual. Switching your candy bowl for a fruit bowl at home has an even greater impact. Instead of supplying the people you love most with food that is unhealthy and drains their energy you can provide them with the fuel that will improve their health and increase their energy. And, most of all, a fruit bowl on your desk or in your home will help you make healthy food choices. When hunger sets in, your impulse will be to reach for an apple instead of milk chocolate bar.

 ACTION STEPS

1. Buy a decent size bowl for your home and each week replenish it with fresh fruit.

2. If you work in an office, buy a bowl for your desk and fill it up with fresh fruit. If other people often eat your fruit ask them if they would like to contribute to the fruit fund and you can buy fruit for them also.

3. If you work in an office ask the person in charge of HR if they would support a fruit bowl in the break room.

4. At home, talk to your family and explain to them why you have made the switch from the candy bowl to a fruit bowl. Explain the 90-10 rule if necessary.

DRINK WATER
INSTEAD OF SODA

My wife likes to remind me that when we met I had several bottles of orange soda in my refrigerator. I drank a lot of soda and very little water back then. She, on the other hand, carried a bottle of water with her wherever she went. Having spent a lot of time together, her habit of drinking water has rubbed off on me. I noticed when I stopped drinking soda and started drinking water instead, I felt better. I had more energy and I actually lost weight. In addition to exercising and eating better, I drank a lot of water and lost 20 pounds.

When we think about our bodies and the differences between water and soda, the choice is clear. Our bodies are made of mostly water, not soda. We all need water to survive and we need a lot of water to thrive. If we go without water for three days we will die; however, I have never heard of anyone dying from lack of Diet Coke. According to Bio-Hydration Research Lab, our bodies use water to provide our cells with life sustaining oxygen and nutrients. Water flushes out carbon dioxide, toxins and other waste products. All of the body's processes are enhanced when we are fully hydrated.

On the other hand, while soda is made up of water, it also contains chemicals, sugar, aspartame (if it's diet) caramel color, phosphoric acid, and other unnatural ingredients that our body doesn't process as well as water. We must remember that our bodies are energy machines and how we fuel it is very important. Like a car, if we fill up with better fuel, our engine works better. In contrast, when we feed our bodies with soda instead of water we don't operate as efficiently or effectively. Our bodies have to work that much harder to process and eliminate the chemicals found in soda from our body. Some studies even indicate that our body holds onto the chemicals from soda in our cell tissue.

When we drink water, we fill up our bodies with the fuel our body craves. Our body wants and needs water—not soda. And when we choose water over soda we feel the difference. According to Ellington Darden, Ph.D., an exercise scientist, water is one of the simplest keys to increased energy and loss of body fat. I believe Dr. Darden calls water a simple key because it is a simple choice. It's as easy as putting money into the drink machine and pushing the water button instead of the soda button.

 ACTION STEPS

1. Chose water instead of soda.

2. Drink sparkling water instead of soda if you want some bubbles.

3. Buy a water filter for your home to drink the best water possible.

4. When choosing bottled water, try to buy purified water.

DRINK SMALL AMOUNTS
OF CHILLED WATER
EVERY 30 MINUTES

Try it now and see how this simple habit refreshes and energizes you. While I briefly discussed this strategy earlier in the book, I felt it was so helpful to me and the people who have tried it that I wanted to share more information about why the simple action of drinking water every 30 minutes will make a big difference.

Studies show that when you consume small amounts of chilled water every 20-30 minutes during the day, you provide a strong, clear and continual signal to your body to keep your energy elevated. In addition, you improve your overall health and resistance to illness. While it is not yet a scientific fact, studies by Dr. Darden, the exercise scientist who has been the director of research for Nautilus Sports/Medical Industries in Colorado Springs, suggest that you get even more energized by drinking ice-cold water than water at room temperature. He says, "A gallon of ice-cold water requires more than 200 calories of heat energy to warm it to core body temperature of 98.6 degrees." This process requires almost one calorie to warm one ounce of cold water to body temperature. Thus, this heat energy that your body creates to warm the cold water provides you with more energy for your life.

Another reason to sip water every 30 minutes is to keep your kidneys fully hydrated. If your kidneys do not get enough water, function is hindered, waste products accumulate and the liver assumes the role of flushing out the impurities. This diverts the liver from its main duty of metabolizing stored fat into usable energy. This means less burning of your body fat and less energy for you. This also explains one of the reasons why drinking plenty of water helps you lose weight and body fat.

Human beings also lose about nine cups of water a day through breathing, perspiration, urination, and bowl movements. And this doesn't include water loss through physical exercise which results in even more water loss. When you sip chilled water every 30 minutes you replenish your water loss and provide your body with more energy for life. Try it now and feel the energy difference.

 ACTION STEPS

1. Befriend a cup or bottle of cold water. If you work at home, keep one in the refrigerator.

2. If you work in an office keep a bottle of water cold with an insulator. Or even bring a mini-cooler of ice with you to work.

3. Sip the water every 30 minutes and energize your body and brain.

VISIT YOUR LOCAL
HEALTH FOOD STORE

This visit will only take an hour but if you have never been to a health food store, the experience will open your eyes to a new and healthy world full of great energy. When I lived in Atlanta, I remember my first visit to a store called Return2Eden and learning there were products that were similar to the ones I would buy in a regular supermarket but were more natural and healthier. Sure, many of these products are a little more expensive, but, with the popularity of stores such as Whole Foods Market and the creation of entire health sections in regular supermarkets it is becoming even easier to find large selections of organic and natural foods at decent prices.

I recommend a visit to a health food store or a mega health food store such as Whole Foods so that you can learn more about natural foods and products that will give you more energy. The people who work at these health food stores are great resources who teach you a lot about the benefits of eating certain foods and vitamins. They can explain what makes certain products better than others. They can also recommend the best vitamins to fit your needs. I learned a great deal about vitamins, nutrition, hydrogenated oils, and organic fruit from the people at these health food stores. Visiting these stores will also teach you to read the ingredients of everything you buy and help you become more conscious of the food you are feeding your body. You will become more educated and empowered to make better choices for your health and energy.

I encourage you to try the products in these stores. You will find that many of the snacks made with the good oils such as expeller pressed oil taste a lot better than the foods with the bad hydrogenated oils. For example, after my many visits to health food stores I now eat Fig Newmans instead of Fig Newtons. Read the ingredients and you'll see a big difference. I eat Smuckers All Natural Peanut Butter with no hydrogenated oil instead of Jiff or Skippy which contains corn syrup and hydrogenated oil. And I eat all-natural cheese instead of processed cheese loaded with chemicals. My first visit to a health food store has made a big difference in my life and I believe it will make a big difference in yours.

RECHARGE YOUR BATTERIES WITH THE ENERGY OF SLEEP

Failure is more frequently from want of energy than want of capital.

DANIEL WEBSTER

I have heard many people say sleep is overrated. That is, until they don't get any of it. While there are a few of us who don't require much sleep most of us require at least eight hours a night and nine to 10 hours a night is optimal, according to Cornell Psychology Professor James B. Maas. Research by Mass shows that if you get less than eight hours of sleep a night, you are operating impaired; your alertness, productivity, creativity, and general health are all affected. We have always heard that driving impaired is a major concern but living impaired is another matter all together. Mass explains that one-third of Americans get six hours of sleep a night or less when they should be getting nine or 10. Indeed, to many, it seems that sleep is extremely underrated.

According to Mass, "Between the seventh and eighth hour of sleep is when we get almost an hour of REM (rapid eye movement) sleep, the time when the mind repairs itself, grows new connections and recharges us. If you only sleep six hours a night, you're missing that last, important opportunity to repair and to prepare for the coming day." This means less energy for your body and less energy for you.

The facts are we need to sleep in order to reenergize our bodies. Our energy bodies need to be refueled and our batteries need to be recharged. Only sleep can do this. Sleep can not be replaced. Studies show without sleep you are prone to more accidents, mistakes, and fatigue. Who wants to live life impaired like this as Mass suggests? And why should we have to? We can make time for sleep. We can sleep at least eight hours and recharge our batteries in order to have more energy for the upcoming day. If you have ever used a cell phone, you know how fast your battery runs out when it isn't charged. Now, we must realize the same goes for us and our internal batteries. Instead of only sleeping six to seven hours a night and operating on half a battery we can sleep eight to 10 hours a night and charge our battery to the max. Here are a few action steps to help you get eight-10 hours of sleep a night.

 ACTION STEPS

1. Decide what time you need to go to bed to get at least eight hours of sleep a night.

2. In your daily planner write down that time and make sure you are in bed 10 minutes before that time. Note the first few nights may be difficult to fall asleep. Keep in mind you are training yourself and your body.

3. To help you go to sleep, avoid sugars and caffeine before bed. Eat a snack if you are hungry. Exercise during the day but not right before bed. Also take a five to 10 walk after dinner to help you sleep deeper at night.

4. Clear your mind and say to yourself, "It's time to go to bed. I deserve to sleep." If your mind starts thinking, use this self talk to help you tune out your thoughts. Also say, "I can think all about this tomorrow. Now is the time for me to sleep." A psychologist taught me this technique 10 years ago and it has worked for me.

5. Just stick to your planner and go to bed each night at

the same time. Eventually you will get used to going to bed at that time.

6. Observe your energy in the morning and throughout the day as you get more sleep each night.

7. For more information on sleeping well visit www.sleep-foundation.org.

TAKE A POWER NAP

My Grandfather Eddy told me that one of the keys to his long and energetic life is a daily short power nap. At 85 years of age he still takes one. While not everyone may need a daily power nap, for those who are not getting enough sleep at night, a power nap will help you refresh your mind and body during the day. Cornell psychologist Dr. James Maas, author of *Power Sleep* writes, a 20 minute nap in the afternoon actually provides more rest than sleeping an extra 20 minutes in the morning. According to Charles McPhee, also known as the "dream doctor," naps should be performed at mid-day—about eight hours after we wake up—so as to not disturb the natural biorhythm of our sleep-wake cycles. He also says, "Naps also should be short, definitely no longer than 30 minutes. (Longer naps allow us to settle into deep sleep, from which it is difficult to awaken)."

While sleep experts are recommending corporations provide nap rooms for their employees to increase their productivity, many bosses do not understand the benefits of a power nap. So what's an Energy Addict, who works in an office, to do when they need to recharge their midday battery? Here are a few Action Steps to help you make a power nap a part of your day when it is needed most.

 ACTION STEPS

1. While others are taking their 20-minute coffee break you take a 20-minute power nap.

2. In advance tell your boss and co-workers that you are going to take a power nap instead of a coffee break. Show them this book or print out the newest research from the National Institute of Mental Health that shows that naps prevent burnout at www.nimh.nih.gov/events/sleep.cfm.

3. The Dream Doctor says not to worry if you don't fall asleep. Just closing your eyes and relaxing peacefully will be refreshing in itself.

4. To prevent you from napping too long, the Dream Doctor recommends you set an alarm for 15-30 minutes on your watch or cell phone. This will also help you rest more peacefully.

5. Lastly, if all else fails the Dream Doctor jokingly recommends the 10 best things to say if you get caught napping at your desk at www.dreamdoctor.com. My two favorites:

≈ "This is just a 15-minute power-nap like they raved about in that time-management course you sent me to."

≈ "I wasn't sleeping! I was meditating on our mission statement."

CREATE YOUR ENERGY ADDICT'S SURVIVING AND THRIVING KIT

I own a small black gym bag that I now call my surviving and thriving kit. Inside this bag, I keep many of my power sources. A box of raisins, a bag of nuts, and a container of trail mix are a few of the healthy snacks I carry with me. My kit also contains a bottle of vitamins, sneakers for walking, two of my favorite books, my favorite movie, my favorite songs on a CD, a box of green tea, a bottle of Penta Water, and a picture of my wife and kids. I consider the contents of this bag fuel for my life. When I am feeling hungry and tired, my snack is within reach. If I forgot to take my vitamins in the morning, they are available in my bag. If I feel sluggish after lunch, a light walk with my sneakers usually does the trick. I never get fatigued from lack of water with my bottle near me and I can always energize my mind with a great book, a cup of green tea, an uplifting song, an inspiring movie or simply a meaningful picture of my wife and kids. My kit is truly a bag full of energy.

I encourage you to create your own Energy Addict's Surviving and Thriving Kit. As an Energy Addict you'll always want the positive, powerful sources of energy you are addicted to within reach. The great thing about an Energy Addict's Surviving and Thriving Kit is we can all create our own customized contents. As you read this book and discover the power sources in your life, you can add them to your kit. This will help you incorporate your power sources into your daily routine and life. At first it may feel funny to create your own, but think of it this way. Doctors need specific instruments to be helpful. Plumbers need their tool kit to be effective. Artists need their paint and paper to create. And

Energy Addicts need great sources of energy to thrive. A Surviving and Thriving Kit helps you bring many of your power sources into one mobile, accessible bag that is available whenever and wherever you need some fuel.

 ACTION STEPS

1. Convert a gym bag or bag of your choice into your Surviving and Thriving Kit.

2. Decide what power sources you would like to add to your kit.

3. Bring your kit to your office or on the road when you are driving or traveling.

4. Whenever you need some fuel, reach into your kit and do what Energy Addicts do best—use great sources of energy to create success in their lives.

USE THE MAGICAL
OFF BUTTON

This simple strategy has helped me escape from my cell...phone that is. Where I once was confined, I now am free because I found the "off" button that liberated me. Think about it. There is nothing in the user's manual that says your phone or pager must stay on 24/7. If you don't want to be bothered during a movie, dinner, at home, or during a conversation, or meeting, just shut the phone off and let your voicemail accept the call. When you are ready to talk, simply turn your phone on, check your messages and call people back on your time instead of theirs. You'll be amazed at how simply shutting off your phone at certain times will help you focus and increase your energy.

When your phone is always ringing and you're doing three things at once your energy is being scattered in many different directions. You can't help but feel uneasy, and stressed out. Your energy doesn't want to be in three different places at once. It wants to be in one place. Shutting off your phone allows you to focus your energy now, on the people you are talking to now, and on the matters that need your attention in front of you now. When you are finished dealing with these situations you can turn your phone back on to handle other situations.

When you first start shutting your phone off you will experience a little separation anxiety, but soon that will be replaced by a new feeling of power. You will look at that "on/off" button and you say, "Wow! I can shut you off when ever I want." Remember that the phone works for you. You don't work for the phone. You don't have to be confined any more. The phone is not a prison. It is a tool for you to communicate when you need to use it. It is meant to make you more successful, not scattered and tired. So don't let your cell phone drain your energy. Shut it off until you are ready to use it.

IGNORE THE
CALL WAITING FEATURE

How many times have we been on a call and we hear the dreaded "beep?" The conversation is interrupted over and over again. I don't know about you but I think it makes people feel unimportant when the person they are talking to checks to see who else is calling. If the person clicks back to us and says, "I have to go," then we are left feeling unimportant. If the person says to the person calling on the other line, "I'll call you back I am talking to so and so," the person calling is likely to feel unimportant. It also takes a lot of energy to maintain several conversations at once. Clickers waste a lot of energy going back and forth from one conversation to another, in many cases for several hours a day. Half the time they can't even remember to whom they are speaking. I have been in the presence of many clickers and they always appear frantic, disorganized and chaotic.

Shouldn't we just reserve the call waiting feature for times when we are waiting for the doctor to call or the real estate agent to say that our house has been sold? Shouldn't we give the person on the other line the attention they deserve? And shouldn't we do it most of all for ourselves and our own energy's sake? Most phone systems have voice mail that will answer when you are on the other line. When we are done speaking we can check our messages and call people back. When you ignore the call waiting feature, you will notice your conversations are more meaningful and you don't feel as scattered. You can focus on one conversation and exchange positive calm energy with the person on the other end of the phone, rather than hurrying from one caller to the next. Try ignoring call waiting for a week and observe how you no longer feel drained after talking on the phone. Hear the difference in your conversations and feel how your focused conversations with one person at a time actually feeds you with energy.

RELAX INSTEAD OF TALK

While we may not be able to control all that happens to us, we can control what happens inside us.

BENJAMIN FRANKLIN

The urge comes over us. We are in the car, sitting in traffic, bored as can be. We reach for the mobile phone or turn on the hands-free phone and make a call. Why? Do we really need to talk or are we just trying to fill the time? An Energy Addict knows the difference. The difference between talking unnecessarily and relaxing is the difference between having energy and losing energy. With each meaningless conversation that's only purpose is to fill time, we leak more energy from our lives and prevent ourselves from tapping the powerful energy inside us.

Perhaps we can think of something else to do instead of talk. How about thinking positive thoughts? Reflecting? Relaxing? After all, we're in a car. Isn't that enough technology to handle at once? We should consider using this time to center ourselves; to take deep breaths and relax; to say our thank you's; to reflect on our professional and personal lives. Instead of talking on the phone to be busy, busy, busy, we can use that time to balance our lives and give ourselves the time and space to energize.

 ACTION STEPS

1. Try this on your next drive. If you don't really need to talk to anyone, shut your phone off and focus on relaxing while you drive.

2. Take deep breaths while you drive. Focus on your breathing.

3. Thank God for the wonderful things in your life.

4. Observe how you feel when you arrive to your destination. Do you have more energy or less?

5. Notice how you are a safer, less aggressive driver when you do this.

6. If you like the results try this again and gain.

TRANSFORM THE ENERGY OF INFORMATION INTO THE POWER OF KNOWLEDGE

I know a CEO named Keith Frein, who hired me to give a seminar to his company, PPR Travel. PPR was recently ranked by Inc. Magazine as the 70th fastest growing company in the United States. After a few discussions with Keith I realized why his company was so successful. Keith is an Energy Addict who helps his people transform the energy of information into the power of knowledge. Information is like gas in a gas tank. It sits passively, waiting to be used, pure potential energy waiting to be tapped. When we go to the gas pump and fill up we transform potential energy into actual energy for our car.

In the same way, when we tap the energy of information we transform it into the power of knowledge. We transform potential energy into actual energy for our life.

In today's world change is not just possible, it is inevitable. You not only need to know about the companies, people, standards and terminology that are dominating the current landscape, but you also need to have an eye on the future. What is coming soon? What could happen five years from now? What could be so disruptive that it changes your entire industry, profession and career or so revolutionary that it changes the way we live? Or what could simply be helpful right now?

Keith knows in today's world, knowledge is power and the more you know the more energy you create. So Keith studies, learns and acquires knowledge. Keith reads books that will help him grow his business. He pays for his company to go to seminars with the thought leaders of the 21st century. He encourages his employees to read books that will help their performance. He reads newspapers, magazines and online magazines that tell him what is happening in his industry, why it is happening and what will happen. Keith knows that he must stay one step ahead of his competition and that one step starts with finding the information and using it to grow his business and his life. Keith is an Energy Addict because he transforms the energy of information into the power of knowledge.

The great thing about information is you don't have to be a CEO to find it. In the information age of today, information is cheap and easy to find. Go to your favorite search engine, type a few key words, and you will have thousands of websites and resources at your fingertips. You don't have to be a CEO or a professional to tap the energy of information. Parents can use the internet to search for parenting tips and safe products. Students use the internet every day to write research papers. Writers like me use the internet to find famous quotes to share with readers. Whatever you want to learn, the information is obtainable. Whatever you want to create, the information is accessible. However you want to grow, the information is available. Whether you are searching to improve your career or your life, finding the necessary information is as easy as going to a gas tank and filling up. Just tap the information, learn it, and transform it into the power of knowledge.

 ACTION STEPS

1. Visit www.google.com and use their advanced search feature to find anything you need. Google was introduced to me several years ago and it is incredible.

2. Read one magazine a month pertaining to your job or career. If you are a full time parent choose a parenting magazine such as *Parenting*.

3. Subscribe to online newsletters that provide information on topics you want to learn more about. Most are free.

GIVE UP THE BAGS

Happiness is good health and a bad memory.

INGRID BERGMAN

Have you ever seen a homeless person walking the street with a cart piled high with a mound of what appeared to be useless stuff? You might have wondered what that person was doing with all that junk. He or she couldn't possibly need all of it. After all, it seemed so pointless for them to carry the cart around with them wherever they went.

Unfortunately, many of us go through life with tons of junk and excess baggage we don't need. We carry around our past with us like a cart of useless stuff that doesn't serve any purpose. Sure, our past has helped us evolve into who we are, but our past is not who we are now. We learn from our past but we are not our past. We are our present.

Too many of us carry excess baggage through our life and this weighs us down like a ton of bricks. This baggage from the past stops us from living energetically, enthusiastically, and joyfully. At times you might say to yourself, "Let it go, it was a long time ago" or "I wish I could just forget about it," but the past stays with you and holds on to you like an anchor keeps a boat in place. Stagnant is what you become and a funk is what your feel. Like a bad dream your legs move really fast but you don't go anywhere.

As we discussed in the energy of now, when your energy is in the past, it cannot be in the present. If you put your thoughts and emotions into the past this means that you have less energy for your life now. Of course you are not going to be as happy, successful and energetic as you could be because you're only using a small portion of your energy to create a healthy body and healthy mind now. The rest of it is in the past. Instead of walking effortlessly you're carrying around these heavy bags that make you walk slow and tired.

While getting rid of your excess baggage is not always easy, the first step is to be conscious you are carrying around the past with you on some level. Maybe you have a few bags or maybe you have a lot of bags. I have coached people who did not even realize they spent most of their day thinking about why nothing in their life has gone right instead of spending their energy on making things right today. Instead of thinking like a winner, they feel like a victim. They think about who has hurt them instead of who can help them now. When I point out the fact all they do is talk about why their life stinks instead of making it great, the realization points them on the road to the present.

I hope reading this helps you become conscious of your thoughts and words. Are you always thinking about the past and feeling like a victim who has been hurt by everyone, or are you someone who has let the past go in order to create your life today? Once you become conscious that you carry too much baggage with you, you can choose to check your baggage at the "counter of the past." Drop them off and let the past do what it wants with them. Consider your life a bus that doesn't allow its passengers to take bags onboard. Bring only yourself, your positive thoughts, your present happiness and enjoy the ride. It will be a light ride filled with no bags and a lot of energy.

ACTION STEPS

1. Determine if you think too much about your past. Do you identify with your past? Do you think too much about the people and events that hurt you? Do you blame others for your current situation? Do you accept responsibility for your life now?

2. Monitor your words and thoughts. When a past thought or emotion pops up, allow yourself to feel it and think it and then let it go. Don't hold on to it. Forgive the people who have hurt you. Look at the past as a learning experience. Be thankful of what you have now.

3. Don't be a victim. While you have been a victim in the past you don't have to be a victim now. You can take control of your energy and your happiness now.

4. Check your bags at the door and let your past go. Focus your thoughts, words, mind and heart on the present. Decide to create your best life today.

BECOME AN ENERGY RECEIVER

In my seminars I suggest to people that they go through life with their heads up, their arms out, and their eyes open. I recommend this because as energy beings we not only share our energy with the world, but we also receive a lot of energy from other people and our higher power. When we are open, the energy will find us. It's like tuning your radio to a great radio station. You adjust the frequency and great music finds it.

Unfortunately many of us put up our energy blockers and stop this flow of energy. Many people go through life with their head down and arms closed. They physically and mentally block energy from entering their space. They don't allow life to bring them wonderful unexpected gifts; strangers and friends are not allowed to get too close; and the positive energy of others is not able to penetrate the shield they have built around their life. They don't want or think they need the help of others. They also don't think anyone would want to help them. They fear, distrust and guard. They build walls to protect themselves, but instead these walls only cut off the supply of energy and lead to a tired and lonely existence. It also takes a lot more energy to keep positive energy out of our lives than it does to let it in.

True success comes when we allow others to share their energy with us. This energy comes in many different forms. I call them gifts of life and gifts from others. When we open our arms to the world we allow ourselves to receive these wonderful gifts from friends, family, strangers and life. Perhaps these gifts come in the form of a returned lost wallet, a door opened, a check in the mail, great advice, a new perspective on life, a smile, or a new job offer. Or perhaps they come in the form of a sunset, an ocean view, an answered prayer, a family gathering. Each day presents a new opportunity to receive the gifts of life and the gifts of others. We should wake up in the morning with curious optimism and ask, "What will life bring me today?" Where in the past we may not have noticed or ignored these gifts, we now need to open our eyes, see all the gifts that life brings and say "thank you" for being blessed. When we allow others to share their energy with us and believe that good things will happen, they always will. When we become an Energy Receiver we tune into a more energetic, open and loving life.

 ACTION STEPS

1. Determine if and how you block yourself from receiving the positive energy of others. Do you turn away advice? Do you think that you don't need anybody? Are you so afraid of being hurt that you don't accept good friends in your life?

2. Determine if you block yourself from receiving the energy of your higher power. Do you pray for guidance? Do you ask for strength and help?

3. Open your doors and allow new people and new friends to come into your life.

4. Be open to other people's ideas and suggestions without feeling threatened. Learn from everyone you meet.

5. Pray for guidance.

CREATE YOUR "YES" LIST AND "NO" LIST

We are what we repeatedly do. Excellence, then, is not an act, but a habit.

ARISTOTLE

Before we go shopping we create a list. Right? We create lists for everything, from wedding lists to to-do lists. They help us categorize and organize to make good choices. So I thought it would be helpful if we created a positive energy list (yes list) and a negative energy list (no list). This will help you organize your power sources and energy drainers into two easily readable lists.

Life is all about habits. Our words, choices, thoughts and actions are all habits. Thinking positive thoughts is just as much a habit as thinking negative thoughts. So if we want to make positive changes in our lives, we have to change our habits. While replacing a bad habit with a good habit takes time and effort, tools such as this energy list will help you make better choices, remember your priorities and keep you on track.

So let's make a list. On a piece of paper, make two columns. On the left side write at the top of the page "Positive Energy." On the top right side of the page write "Negative Energy." Then simply write down the power sources, under positive energy, that energize your life. Whether you have been incorporating these power sources into your life or whether you want to make them a new habit, write them down. While you may have a few good habits today, this list, will also help you maintain these habits. Under positive energy you might write something like "Eat fruits and vegetables," "Think positive thoughts" and "Drink more water." Under negative energy you might write something like "yelling at family and employees," "gossiping" and "eating fast food."

Since it is your life, I don't want to create your list for you. But to help you create your list I am going to show you a short version of mine. I use this list often. If I want to have that big tasty chocolate chip cookie and I already ate my 10 percent worth of treats for the week, I look down at my list and under the negative energy list I see CHOCOLATE CHIP COOKIE. Big capital letters. This helps me not to eat it even though a little voice is saying "you want it."

POSITIVE ENERGY	NEGATIVE ENERGY
Say positive affirmations	Thinking negative thoughts
Eat fruits, vegetables, raisins & nuts	Being judgmental
Exercise daily	Draining other people's energy
Eat a healthy breakfast	Yelling at my children
Give compliments to my employees	Eating unhealthy fast food
Play with my children	Being controlling
Be patient with others	Thinking too much about the future
Get at least 8 hours of sleep	Feeling stressed
Take energizing breaths	CHOCOLATE CHIP COOKIE

 **ACTION STEPS**

1. Create your list as long or short as you want it.

2. Write this list on a piece of paper that you carry in your pocket. Also have a copy of this list in your car.

3. Tape this list to your mirror.

4. Wherever you go you will want to see this list to help you make good choices and develop great habits. Remember you are the energy that you fuel your life with.

5. Use the ritual planner on page 16 to help you incorporate your yes list into your life.

TAP YOUR SHARE
OF INFINITY

---

*You are never given a wish without also being given
the power to make it true.*

RICHARD BACH

No one really knows how big the universe is. In fact, there are theories that it is expanding infinitely. We have theories but no one really knows for sure. No matter what the scientists approximate, we can all agree that the universe is big. Really big. And if we know the universe is big we must also assume that there is a whole lot of energy in the universe—and there is.

The way I see it, God is a BIG GOD with a lot of energy. Perhaps an infinite amount of energy. This energy makes the world go around. It lights up the stars and fuels every living creature on earth. With so much energy in the universe, and with such a big God, I often wonder why as energy beings many of us expect so little of ourselves and the world around us. A friend of mine says God is going to do new things so we have to do new things. God is not stagnant, so we can't be stagnant. And in order for God to do new things God works through us—through people like Mother Teresa, Einstein and Martin Luther King Jr. and through musicians, writers, doctors, teachers, and through people like you and me.

As an Energy Addict we must tap our share of infinity. There is so much energy in the universe even if we tap a big share, there will still be plenty of energy for everyone else. It's like going to a Super Wal-Mart and loading your cart with stuff. The store is so big the amount you buy won't even make a dent on the shelves. So don't be afraid to tap your share of energy. God wants you to have it and wants you to use it.

Don't be afraid to ask for more energy than you think you deserve. You deserve everything you need. You are a shining star and you need lots of energy to shine your light. This doesn't mean that you are greedy. It means that whatever you want to create in your life you can expect to have the energy to make it happen. You are not afraid to ask God for what you need to do great things in this world. You realize when you expect more, you get more and you do more.

Make this moment the last time you think a dream will not happen. Don't ever say again, "I just don't think I can do it" or "It probably won't happen." If this is what you expect, this is what you will get. Instead, tap your share of infinity. There's plenty of energy so why shouldn't you ask for your share? Believe God and the universe will provide you with all the energy you will ever need to accomplish your goals and live your dreams. Understand this energy comes in many ways and takes many forms. It may come in the form of a mentor to help you win that promotion you have been working for. Or $100,000 loan for a new start-up business. Advice that puts you on the right path. Support that gets you through a tough time. Expert advice when it is needed most. Money that helps you pay your over due bills. Or a person that introduces you to a number of people that help make your career or business prosper.

The energy is infinite and to tap it we have to believe great things will happen and we have to put our energy out into the world to make them happen. We can expect less, do less and create less, or we can expect more, do more and create more. By believing great things will happen, we create a pipeline to our source of infinite energy. By taking action, we say to God we're making it happen so send us some energy. God then opens the pipeline and sends us the energy we need. I see this happen all the time in my own life and in the lives of many others. I hope you will try to tap your share of infinity as well. To guide you in this process, try the following action steps.

ACTION STEPS

1. Decide what you want to do or create. What is your goal?

2. Pray for guidance. Ask God for the strength, energy and resources to accomplish your goal.

3. Expect God will provide you with the resources you need. Don't even doubt it for a second. Believe that it is happening right now.

4. Take action. Put all of your energy in the present moment to reach your goal. Set the wheels in motion. Put your energy out there.

5. Watch how the pipeline opens and you receive your share of infinity.

PROJECT THE ENERGY THAT "EVERYTHING HAPPENS FOR A REASON"

Seekers are offered clues all the time from the world of the spirit. Ordinary people call these clues coincidences.

DEEPAK CHOPRA

As Chopra says, ordinary people call these clues coincidences. Energy Addicts call them "signs of grace." The funny thing about signs of grace is, at the time, you can't read them. You know they mean something and that is the important thing but the sign becomes clearer when you look back at your life. A friend recently told me the well-known story of the farmer who had a son and a horse. People said, "That's great you have a son and a horse." The farmer said, "Could be good, could be bad." One day the horse ran away and everyone said that was bad. The farmer said, "Could be good or could be bad." Then the horse came back with five more horses. Everyone said this was good. The farmer said, "Could be good, could be bad." While the son was training one of the horses, it threw him and the son broke both his legs. Everyone said this was bad. The farmer said, "Could be good, could be bad." The next day the army came to take his son away to fight in the Civil War. He couldn't go because both legs were broken.

The truth is we never know at the time why things happen the way they do. But when we look back there is always a reason for everything. Where I used to get upset about negative things that happened to me, I now choose to put out the energy that everything happens for a reason, and I find all the time that it does. We have two choices. We can look at problems and negative events as problems and negative events or as learning experiences and signs of grace.

When I ran for the city council of Atlanta in 1997, I was

running against a 20-year incumbent and several formidable challengers. I walked to 7,000 houses door to door during the campaign and was actually scaring everyone in the race. I came out of nowhere in my first election and was clearly leading. Then one of the candidates started to attack me with lies and negative campaigning in the hopes she would beat me and make it into the run-off with the incumbent. Her strategy worked, as I did not have enough money to counter the negative campaigning. When I lost the election I was crushed. I felt like a victim. Looking back I now realize that everything happened for a reason. If I would have won the election, I would have most likely stayed in Atlanta. I would have never moved with my family to the beach and I would not be on the path I am on today. The signs of grace pointed me in the right direction and while I didn't know it then, I see it very clearly now.

When we look at every situation as a sign of grace we live more energetically and calmly. We flow through life and allow our purpose and destiny to unfold. We don't treat every situation as the end of the world. Instead of fighting everything that happens we accept these experiences and learn from them. In fact, the more we believe everything happens for a reason the more we start to look for signs of grace. When something happens, we say like the farmer, "Could be good and could be bad." We think, "I wonder where this will lead me." And like the farmer's story, when we believe everything happens for a reason our story always has a positive, happy ending.

👟 ACTION STEPS

1. Think about a time in your life when you thought something bad happened but it turned out to be a blessing.

2. Write down each experience and keep this on hand. When uncertainty happens in your life you can refer to these experiences.

LEARN YOUR
LIFE LESSONS

The trouble I have with you is me.

MICHAEL HUSKEY

Do you have events and situations that keep coming up in your life? Do you have a recurring theme such as issues with control, trust, acceptance and love? They play over and over again in your life like a broken record. I call these recurring problems life lessons and they will present themselves throughout our lives if we do not address them. I have found when you seek to learn from your problems, they don't come up anymore. In fact when you see a problem as a learning experience instead of a problem, the problem disappears. However, if we avoid our life lessons they will continue to appear in our lives, over and over again, causing unnecessary stress, draining our energy, and creating unhappiness.

For example, throughout the first few years of my marriage I struggled with control issues. I always wanted to control everything. Have you ever felt this way? At the time, I saw everything as her fault. She was making me frustrated by letting the repair man charge her too much. It was her fault for not planning dinner. She was to blame for getting into a fender bender. Only when I faced my life lesson of "control" and not being able to let go, did everything begin to change. I focused my energy on dealing with this issue. I realized that the problem wasn't my wife; the problem was me. Sure enough, when a few situations arose that would normally trigger my control issues, I let my wife handle the situation. Rather than blaming her, I supported her during the process. Not only did she feel more empowered in her life, I felt more empowered in mine. The amazing thing is once I learned my life lesson, control issues stopped appearing. While other life lessons still appear from time to time, I take each one in stride and identify what I can learn from them. Then I learn and they disappear.

When we treat our problems as life lessons and learning experiences we replace an enormous amount of negative energy with positive energy. Instead of wasting energy on a problem we create energy by developing a solution. By facing our life lessons we eliminate any power certain issues have over us. We, in essence, shine a light on our problems and because negative energy can't survive in the light, they disappear. This eliminates the energy blockages they cause in our lives and we are free to flow on, happier and more energetic.

You can identify your life lessons by observing the reoccurring theme in your life. For instance, have several of your dating partners said the same things about you? Could be a life lesson. At work do you get into the same arguments with different people? Your life lesson is calling you. Or perhaps you and your significant other have the same argument over and over again. It's time to learn your life lesson. When you do you will spend less energy solving your problems than dealing with them all the time. This will free up your energy for everything else.

👟 ACTION STEPS

1. Identify your life lessons. What issues keep on appearing? Look in the mirror and determine what you need to learn.

2. Be conscious of your life lesson and seek to change your pattern of behavior when confronted with a life lesson situation.

3. Observe that when you have effectively learned your life lesson they don't come back.

4. Be on the lookout for another life lesson. You never know when they will appear.

5. Think of every problem as a learning experience and free up your energy.

LET IT FLOW

There is an appointed time for everything. And there is a time for every event under heaven; A time to give birth, and a time to die; A time to plant and a time to uproot what is planted.

ECCLESIASTES 3:1-2

The universal law of impermanence says nothing lasts forever. People live and die. Thoughts come and go. Wounds eventually heal. Mistakes are finally forgotten. Success and fame come to an end. Even the sun will stop shining at some point. We live in a changing universe where energy flows from one form to another. The seasons teach us there is a time for everything. In the summer the energy flows to produce bountiful harvests and crops. In autumn, the energy of creation slowly leaves the land as it prepares for winter to recharge. Then winter comes and the land in essence hibernates and reenergizes itself. The land stores up and maximizes its energy to get ready to give life once again in the spring. In the springtime energy flows to create vibrancy and liveliness that will lead to a fruitful summer. Each season is essential to the other. And each moment in our life is essential to living the next.

In each moment we have an opportunity to control or let it flow. Knowing nothing lasts forever it makes it easier not to get attached to anything. It doesn't mean we don't enjoy what we have. We just don't get attached to it because we know like us, it too, will cease to exist, and the energy will flow into another state and another form. In fact, we enjoy what we have much more because knowing we will not have it forever makes us enjoy it more now. Like a child who only has one day to play with a toy, we make the most of what we have, when we have it. And like our land that transforms with each new season, we are transformed by the energy that flows through us.

We all will go through cycles in our lives. One month we will feel creative and the next we'll feel reflective. One day we're happy and the next we're sad. In my life I have experienced times of surging active energy and other times I have felt like a bear in hibernation. Yet I realize that each time is as important as the other. We often have to reflect and recharge in order to create. In solitude we can generate energy that can be shared with others during our season of vibrant energy. Sometimes we have to uproot a part of ourselves so that a new life can begin. Sometimes we have to go through the darkness of winter to experience the lightness of spring. In times of surging energy we need to be active and vibrant, or else the energy will fester inside us. During our times of low energy we need to restore and renew ourselves. We know the seasons will change and so will everything in our life.

The key to maximize your energy is to let the energy flow in and out of your life, from moment to moment and season to season. Don't fight the flow. Fighting the flow of energy is like not allowing the land to go through winter. Without the ability to renew itself, the land will lose all of its energy and lay barren. By not fighting the flow we have more energy when we need it. The land does not fight winter. But accepts it as a time to renew itself. We must accept how we feel when we feel it. We know everything will come and go, so we must embrace it and let it flow.

👟 ACTION STEPS

1. Think of yourself as a ray of light that everything flows through. Things go through you, then back through you. You don't hold onto anything. You just enjoy the time.

SMELL A LITTLE ENERGY

Smell is a potent wizard that transports us across thousands of miles and all the years we have lived.

HELEN KELLER

Have you ever smelled the autumn air and have it remind you of specific time in your past? Or have you ever noticed someone's perfume or cologne and it reminded you of a past relationship? If your answer is "yes" to either question you have experienced the power of smell in your life. According to Dr. Cooper, "The sense of smell is so powerfully connected to the brain that some scents elicit pronounced changes in energy, emotions, and memory." Cooper also states, "Researchers at Harvard Medical School's Institute for Circadian Physiology report growing evidence the power of smell can, at least in some cases, strongly influence mental alertness."

Study after study demonstrates the power of smell. At Rensselaer Polytechnic Institute, researchers showed people who work in pleasantly scented areas performed 25 percent better than those who were in unscented areas. The people in pleasantly scented rooms carried out their tasks more confidently and more efficiently. Tests at the University of Cincinnati indicate fragrances added to the atmosphere of a room can help keep people more alert and improve performance of routine tasks.

So now that we understand that smell can affect our energy, the next question is what smells energize us. According to Cooper, "To date, the top scent for raising energy and attention seems to be peppermint, but lemon is also effective." Cooper recommends the following action steps to determine which scent will give us the best charge of energy. Then all we have to do is smell a little energy when we need it.

👟 ACTION STEPS

1. At different times, try a cup of peppermint tea and lemon tea. Take in the strong fragrant vapors and see which one has the stronger effect. Drink the tea that energizes you the most.

2. Open a bottle of peppermint extract and lemon extract at different times. Whichever pleases your senses the most is the right one for you.

3. Once you decide which smell energizes you the most then consider using a scent dispenser to dispense all-natural essential oils wherever you work or live.

4. Also consider bringing fresh flowers or potpourri into your home or work areas. These natural scents often have a pleasant effect on us.

5. The smell of rosemary is also reportedly effective for uplifting energy and enhancing memory. However, rosemary shouldn't be used by women who are pregnant or anyone with high blood pressure.

DISCOVER YOUR
SECOND BRAIN

I feel there are two people inside me—me and my intuition. If I go against her,
she'll screw me every time, and if I follow her, we get along quite nicely.

KIM BASINGER

If you have ever had butterflies before speaking to a group of
people, a nervous knot in your stomach, or made a split second decision without thinking you have experienced the
energy of your gut—-and this energy is always telling you
something if you listen. When I say "gut," I am referring to
the enteric nervous system that lives inside our intestines.
The gut, or as scientists call it "our second brain," consists of
about 100 million neurons, more than our spinal chord. Our
second brain is an extremely complex system of nerve cells,
neurochemicals that are independent but also interconnected to the brain in our head. According to the National
Institute for Science Education, scientists believe from an
evolutionary purpose the brain in our stomach was first to
form because our primitive ancestors were more interested
in eating to survive than thinking about what clothes they
should wear for the hunting party. When thinking became
more important, the brain in the head developed but the
brain in the gut still remained. In fact, both brains actually
originate from a structure called the neural crest, which
appears and divides during fetal development to and from
both of our brains. The complex physical, chemical and energetic system of the gut enables us to think and act inde-
pendently of the brain while still influencing the way we
think, feel and act.

I share this information with you because the energy of
the gut is another power source that can significantly

improve the way we interact and excel in the world if we choose to listen to it. Even the military has realized the power of gut. In a November 2002 issue of *Business 2.0 Magazine*, an article described a profound experiment. Because of frustrations with the results of rational decision making process of the military during combat and simulations, Paul Van Riper, a retired Marine Corps lieutenant general, brought a group of Marines to the New York Mercantile Exchange in 1995, because the jostling, confusing pits reminded Van Riper of war rooms during combat. The article states:

> First the Marines tried their hand at trading on simulators, and to no one's surprise, the professionals on the floor wiped them out. A month or so later, the traders went to the Corps's base in Quantico, Va., where they played war games against the Marines on a mock battlefield. The traders trounced them again—and this time everyone *was* surprised. When the Marines analyzed the humbling results, they concluded that the traders were simply better gut thinkers. Thoroughly practiced at quickly evaluating risks, they were far more willing to act decisively on the kind of imperfect and contradictory information that is all you ever get in war. Today the Corps official doctrine reads, "The intuitive approach is more appropriate for the vast majority of ... decisions made in the fluid, rapidly changing conditions of war when time and uncertainty are critical factors, and creativity is a desirable trait."

Every day our gut sends us messages that can help us in our life. To tap into the energy of the gut we have to be willing to both listen to it and ask it questions. Is this person friend or foe? Should I do this business deal? Is this house a good investment? Is this a dangerous situation? Is this the right time to make the pitch? When making a critical decision, ask your gut what it thinks and listen for the answer. Your second brain actually will have already given you an answer—even before you ask the question. You just have to remember what it told you before you started to analyze the situation with the brain in your head. Just remember your gut response is the first response you feel before you think something. As you practice doing this you will become more skilled at automatically making decisions with your gut, and questions and answers will happen simultaneously without effort. Discovering and using your second brain will allow you to use another power source to fuel your life with decisions that benefit your health and well being.

 ACTION STEPS

1. Do a gut check every time you are in a high pressure or tense situation. Communicate with your gut and feel what it is telling you.

2. Practice making decisions with your gut in various situations, under high pressure and normal conditions. The more you practice, the better you will become.

3. For a week, when making decisions write down your gut decision and then write down your rational decision after you had time to think. If they were different write which one turned out better. If they were the same write down how you felt about the results. These exercises will help you train yourself to use your gut.

TRUST YOUR GUT

Trusting your intuition means tuning in as deeply as you can to the energy you feel, following that energy moment to moment, trusting that it will lead you where you want to go and bring you everything you desire.

SHAKTI GAWAIN

Can you think of a time in your life when you didn't listen to your gut and wished you did? That inner voice that told you to do something and you said, "You don't know what you're talking about," and used your thinking mind instead. Looking back you say, "I knew I should have listened to my gut." It's happened to me many times. The important thing about these experiences is we know our gut was trying to tell us something. Experiencing moments where we have felt its presence but have ignored its power is still an enormous gift because, if we look back and know we should have listened to our gut, then each one of us also knows that we have the ability to tap into the intuitive energy inside us. All we have to do is listen to it and trust it the next time.

When we learn to listen and trust our inner voice we tap into a source of great wisdom and power. Instead of listening to the fear and doubts often brought about by the rational, thinking mind, our inner voice points us in the direction of our greatest good. This inner voice consists of messages from our gut or second brain and from the energy the great spiritual teachers call our inner knowing or being—that energy inside us that is connected to the infinite energy in the universe or "God" or "higher power." Whatever we call this energy, when we go deep within and connect to this source, our lives will become a miraculous and thrilling ride.

Can you think of times when you heard this mysterious voice whisper something to you, giving you direction, telling you what changes to make, or yelling "get out of here, you're not safe?" I remember many special moments like this and perhaps one of my stories will help you remember the whispers in your life. I was playing a lacrosse game in high school. We were down by one goal with a minute left. The game decided who went to the playoffs. I picked up a ground ball on our end of the field. I began to run down the field to try to score the tying goal. At one point two people came running at me and we all fell down. I remember my mind saying, "You just blew it. It's over." But then I heard this whisper. It didn't come from my mind or my mouth. I remember feeling like time had stopped. The whisper said, "Get up, get up, keep going." Somehow the two people fell on both sides of me and I got up right in between them. I picked the ball back up off the ground and ran towards the goal. With about 10 seconds in the game I jumped in the air, got hit by a few people, fell forward and just threw the ball at the goal as I slammed face down into the ground. Having watched the video tape, I know the ball hit the ground and bounced sharply past the goalie into the top of the net inside the goal. We tied the game.

I always remembered that inner voice telling me to "get up." It happened to me again in college when we beat West Point in overtime. It happened to me when a strange man approached me, my friends and family after an Atlanta Braves game. It happened when a whisper said, "Watch out," and I avoided a car accident.

If you have experienced similar experiences then you know the power of your inner voice. Now all you have to do is trust it and trust often. Be open to the messages and follow them on an exciting journey. I always have fun listening to what my inner voice has to say. And now that I am open to it, and trust it, it has become a part of every decision and success in my life. Practice trusting your gut and observe how you bring more energy and success into your life.

ACTION STEPS

1. Remember a time in your life when your gut told you something and you didn't listen.

2. Think about what stopped you. Usually it is fear or the fact you are trying to please others instead of yourself.

3. The next time you hear your inner voice, listen to it and trust it. Put the fear aside and do what you want to do not what others want you to do.

ELIMINATE CLUTTER: INSIDE AND OUT

Do you have a new project that needs to get done? Perhaps it's a new proposal for a client or the first chapter of the book you have always wanted to write. Maybe it's a new song that has been floating in your head or a plan for your new business. If there is something that you need to do but it's not getting done, one of the first places to start is to clear out the clutter around you and inside you. Clutter can block precious new energy from flowing into your life by filling up your space and life with old stagnant energy that loves to build up and stay right where it is. Clutter in your life might include a messy house, a pile of papers on your desk, mail spread out all over the counter, a closet filled with old clothes you never wear or old salad dressings in your refrigerator.

Whether you attack that to-do list, go through your piles of paper, clean up your desk, or throw out the trash in your car, you clear the physical energy around you and allow new energy to flow in. This simply makes you feel better. It's an energy thing. We are energy and when we free up old stagnant energy around our space we feel more lively and energized.

The same goes for mental clutter. When you get rid of toxic thoughts, toxic people and toxic beliefs in your life you eliminate the energetic clutter that holds you back. Just like Cheryl Richardson says in her best selling book, *Life Makeovers,* if you don't need it and it serves no useful purpose, then "throw it out" and replace it with new and useful energy. Where acupuncture helps eliminate the energy blockages in our body and enables a healthy flow of energy throughout, we have to apply a form of mental acupuncture to free up the energetic clutter in our life. Replace beliefs such as "Bad things always happen to me" with "I accept all the great things in my life." Replace thoughts like "I hate the rain" to "I love the rain because it brings us water and life." This is one I have worked on a lot. And to the people who are always being negative to you and filling your life with negative words and actions, ask them to change. Try to help them change. If they are unwilling you just might have to throw them and their clutter out of your life.

This is your life and you deserve to clear the clutter whenever you feel your energy suffering. Once you clear your clutter you will feel more energized and alive. You will have new energy to start your project and create new success in your life. Try it and you'll feel the difference.

 ACTION STEPS

1. Pick one space in your house and/or office that is cluttered. Organize it and throw out the clutter. Observe how you feel when you are finished.

2. Identify one toxic person, thought or belief in your life and throw out the clutter. Feel how your energy increases.

3. Keep a journal to help release clutter from your mind.

4. Read the books *Clear Your Cutter with Feng Shui* by Karen Kingston and *Organizing From the Inside Out* by Julie Morganstern.

5. Visit www.juliemorgenstern.com and www.overhall.com for ideas about clearing out your clutter.

MAKE TONIGHT YOUR NIGHT

The difference between one man and another is not mere ability it is energy.

THOMAS ARNOLD

You have had a long day. All you feel like doing when you get home is crashing on the couch. After all, this is what you usually do. But then someone like me comes along and says it doesn't have to be this way. I ask you if you would like to have more energy in the evening. You say "yes." I ask you if you would rather be active than sitting on a couch in the evening. You say, "Yes. If only I had the energy I would be more active." Well, there are a few simple changes or additions to your evening routine that can make all the difference. Here are a few action steps to make tonight your night.

ACTION STEPS

1. Eat an energizing snack before dinner. According to William Nagler, MD, psychiatrist at the University of California, Los Angeles School of Medicine, evidence indicates simple hunger-related tensions contribute to fading energy, negative emotions and late-day arguments. When you eat a snack before dinner you will most likely be in better spirits and eat less for dinner. If you are like me and you get very irritable when you don't eat, this strategy will improve your life significantly.

Examples of healthy snacks include: fruit, soup, slice of whole grain bread and low fat yogurt.

2. Create a buffer zone. Take 15—20 minutes to be by yourself after walking in the door before having conversations about personal, financial or professional matters. According to Dr. Cooper, evidence suggests over half of the most damaging arguments are started or magnified within 15 minutes of people greeting each other at the end of the day. This makes sense when you think about how you feel at the end of the day. If you walk in the door and your significant other hits you with a list of bills that need to be paid you are likely to get into an argument. Now I know why my mother said, "Don't talk to your father until he has eaten dinner." When we take the time to walk in the house, get comfortable and then engage in conversations and family time, we will likely have less stressful arguments.

3. Eat smaller dinners. Eat enough to satisfy you but not so much that you want to go to bed after eating.

4. Take a light 10-minute walk after dinner. Instead of plopping down to watch TV take a walk. Walking after dinner, within a half-hour time frame is like pouring gasoline on a fire. It exponentially increases your metabolism and gives you a double boost of energy according to Bryant Stamford, Ph.D., exercise physiologist at the University of Louisville. You will also likely eat less high fat foods and be in a better mood.

5. Play at night. Do some effortless gardening, or play with your kids or pet. Playing at night helps us combat fatigue and stress.

6. Reflect. Think about all the things you are thankful for and say "thank you." I like to go outside and look at the stars (a benefit of living at the beach is that you can see them) and think about how lucky I am to be alive.

START AN
ENERGY ADDICT'S CLUB

---

*Never doubt that a small group of thoughtful, committed citizens can change
the world. Indeed, it's the only thing that ever has.*

MARGARET MEAD

There are many groups and organizations that support people in their struggle with bad relationships, substance abuse,
addictions, deaths and diseases. While these groups and
organizations serve a wonderful purpose in society, I think it
would be a great idea to create a support group to help each
other fuel our lives with positive energy and positive habits.
There are support groups that help people deal with addictions, so why can't there be support groups that help people
become addicted to positive energy?

Imagine a group of people getting together once a week or
once a month and discussing ways to improve each other's
lives. Imagine sharing positive energy and success stories, as
each person learns new strategies and tips. Envision the difference you will make to the people who are just getting started. Visualize a person struggling with getting rid of their negative belief system and you helping this person. As an Energy
Addict you can help them become an Energy Addict, and so on
and so on. The legacy you can leave doing this is enormous.
Imagine the energy this group will create in your town or city.
Envision the power of a group of positive people who are
addicted to positive energy. What benefit will this have on the
community? And imagine this group increasing the physical,
mental and spiritual energy of each of its members, its members' families, friends and co-workers. Think about people like
you and me starting this club at work or in our community.

OK, enough convincing. Let's get started. If you are

interested in starting an Energy Addict's Club, take the following steps.

👟 ACTION STEPS

1. Consider how an Energy Addict's Club gets started and functions. While each club will be different, here are a few suggestions:

≈ A few people and I decided to start the group. We decided to hold monthly meetings and weekly phone calls. We then invited various people to our monthly meeting. At first we met at someone's house and then moved it to anther venue. Your venue could be a church, school, banquet room in a restaurant, etc.

≈ At each meeting, each member would stand up, say their name and say "I am an Energy Addict. I have been an Energy addict for _____ amount of time." Visitors would introduce themselves and say why they were there.

≈ The meeting might consist of different items on the agenda. Perhaps someone shares a personal growth story. A speaker may come and share new insights. And during each meeting the group discusses one or more tips to increase your physical, mental and spiritual energy. Members share how they have incorporated this tip or how they plan to incorporate this tip into their life. They might discuss obstacles that came up and how they overcame them. Tips are taken from this book or new tips are developed and offered by the members.

2. Email me at jon@jongordon.com or call 904.285.6842 and we will guide you through the process. It's very easy and of course there is no charge. Together we will spread positive energy.

SPONSOR SOMEONE

If you can't feed a hundred people, then feed just one.

MOTHER TERESA

A significant component of any addiction group is the concept of a sponsor. A sponsor is there to support someone through the process of their recovery. The sponsor has been through the program and can offer personal experiences that guide and support the person as they face various obstacles. As an Energy Addict you can offer a great deal of wisdom, insight and experience to others as they then become addicted to positive energy. Your energy is contagious and by working with others as a sponsor you can help them increase their energy. You can help them focus to create what matters most. And you can help them discover simple, powerful ways they can energize their life.

The key is to sponsor only the people who want to be sponsored. Just like AA, you can only help people who want to help themselves. Simply ask someone if they would like to have more energy in their life. Most people will say "yes." The next step is to tell them they should read this book. Give them a copy of your book or tell them to go to the library and check it out. Or buy one for them if you can afford it. Or recommend they buy one. While I would like each person to have their own book as a reference, my mission is to help people energize their life. To me it doesn't matter how people come to read this book; I just want them to read it. I certainly don't want money to be an obstacle to someone improving their life.

If they decide to read the book, ask this person if they

would like your support and help during their process of becoming an Energy Addict. Tell them they can ask your advice anytime. And when you give advice you do so with compassion without feeling or acting superior. It's important to let the person know that you have been though this process and you understand the significant changes they are making in their life. As the person becomes an Energy Addict you are there to support, guide and advise them. They will feel your energy and support and will likely reach new heights because of you.

In turn this person will be equipped to sponsor someone else. Eventually we will have Energy Addicts around the country living and helping others live a life filled with positive energy and positive habits. It all starts with becoming an Energy Addict ourselves. Then we can make a difference by sponsoring someone else.

LEAD WITH YOUR HEART

The seat of the soul is to be sought in the heart.

ARISTOTLE

When I speak to various groups I ask people to point to themselves. Almost everyone points at their heart. That's because our heart is our power center. Our heart is who we are. We are energetic beings with an electromagnetic field within our bodies. Within this electromagnetic field are a heart, a brain, and other organs that run on electrical impulses and energy. According to Dr. Robert Cooper, research shows the body's trillions of cells are strongly influenced by the heart which generates energy and is in turn, energized by huge electrical fields that engage us with life. In fact, studies show that the heart's electromagnetic field is approximately 5,000 times greater than the field produced by the brain.

Unfortunately most of us lead with our head when we should be leading with our heart. Think about it. People don't say, "she puts her head into her work." They say, "She puts her heart into her work." The truth is you can't accomplish anything meaningful in your life without putting your heart into it. Try working at a job without putting your heart into it and you will not last long. Not only will you feel it, but others will be able to see it as well. Try creating something your heart doesn't really want, and it won't happen. A relationship won't last long if you don't put your heart into it. When we lead from the heart, everyone can see it and feel it. Most importantly, so can we.

When your heart and mind are in alignment you become an unstoppable force. Your heart leads with tremendous power and your mind follows with positive thoughts, words and energy. When you lead from your heart you live a life filled with purpose and enthusiasm. Going through the motions doesn't cut it anymore. Your life matters and you look forward to springing out of bed in the morning to enjoy the day. You are filled with an intense force of life that emanates from your mouth, your heart and your eyes. Like flies drawn to a light, people are attracted to your energy. They want to hear what you have to say. They want to feel your energy. And they want to look into your eyes. The power of your heart pours through every waking breath and each sleeping dream and fuels your life with the energy to lead an amazing and meaningful life.

 ACTION STEPS

1. Identify what your heart wants. What does your heart want to do and where does it want you to go? To answer this ask yourself meaningful questions such as:

≈ What do I love to do?
≈ What matters to me?
≈ What is my dream?
≈ What do I feel passionate about?
≈ Who do I love and who loves me?

2. Determine if you put your heart into your work or your life. Do you live with a purpose and do you have enthusiasm for what you do? If you don't have a sense of purpose now, can you find it in your current work? Purpose can be derived from anything. I once had an employee who made burritos for a living. I asked the person if they liked being a cook. The person said, "I'm not a cook. I am someone who feeds people so they can live." Purpose is all about perspective. When my wife refers to her job as the caretaker of our children, she says she is

not just raising her children. She is raising them to be future leaders and healers. To me her job is filled with the ultimate purpose.

3. If you can't find a sense of purpose in your current work consider finding a job or career that gives you a sense of purpose. Perhaps you can request a different job within the same company. Or seek out people you admire and find out what they do. What jobs are you naturally attracted to? Start here.

4. Read the books, *The Heart of a Leader* by Ken Blanchard; *Gung Ho! Turn On the People in Any Organization* by Ken Blanchard and Sheldon Bowles and *Fish! A Remarkable Way to Boost Morale and Improve Results* by Stephen C. Lundin, Harry Paul and John Christensen. These books are incredible resources for finding purpose and meaning in your work and life.

COMMUNICATE FROM
THE HEART

The light that shines in the eyes is the light of the heart.

RUMI

Would you like to have more meaningful relationships? Would you like to bring more energy into your relationships? I think we all do. Most studies report we long for more intimate connections. In a world getting smaller and faster by the minute, we are finding it more difficult to connect meaningfully with other people. Unfortunately this is because we are so busy we forget to tap into the energy of our heart. Most of our relationships are based on communicating mind to mind, voice to voice and head to head, without any heartfelt feeling or emotion into our conversations. We are not giving each other the time or the chance to connection meaningfully.

Real communion and communicating happens when we speak heart to heart. According to Dr. Cooper, (you'll notice I quote him a lot because he did such a wonderful job researching our various energy sources), researchers have discovered heartbeats are more than mechanical pump pulses; they actually have an intelligent "energy language" that influences how we perceive and relate to the world. Each and every heartbeat is linked to our thinking brain and to the parts of our nervous system that continually influence our perceptions and awareness. Our heart is continually trying to send us messages if we choose to listen.

When we do listen, we tap into our true power center. According to research published in the *American Journal of Cardiology*, the heart's magnetic field not only permeates every cell in the body but also radiates outward. In fact, electrophysiological changes in feelings transmitted by the heart have been detected up to five feet. This means that if I am standing two to three feet away from you I can feel your heart's energy—your powerful magnetic field—and you can feel mine. That's why it is so important you say what you feel. Otherwise we can tell the difference. That's why we know if someone is being sincere or fake. We can feel it. We can see it. We can read their energy. Someone can say, "I wish you all the best" and we will know whether they mean it or not.

To communicate from the heart, make sure your heart and your mind are aligned. Make sure you say and think what you feel. Helen Keller said, "The best and most beautiful things in the world cannot be seen or even touched...They must be felt with the heart." Each day we can feel the energy of our heart and tap into it to be more real, honest, sincere and compassionate. Or we can ignore its presence and act superficial and artificial. You know the kind of "fake" I am talking about: where someone you know smiles at you, asks how you are doing and doesn't listen to your answer. The kind of phony, surface level conversations that permeate many cocktail parties and office break rooms. While others may be doing this, you can take the path more meaningfully traveled. You can bring more energy into your life and into your relationships by communicating from the heart and trying the following Action Steps.

🥾 ACTION STEPS

1. Engage in meaningful conversations and develop trusting relationships. You'll be amazed at the benefits you receive in the form of advice, life lessons and positive energy when you spend the time to really talk to people and create real bonds of communication. People often marvel at my wife because when she talks to you she gets

right to your heart. Like Barbara Walters, people pour out their heart and they cry together. It's no surprise she has many close friends.

2. Practice empathy. Peter Drucker, Ph.D. says, "The number-one practical competency for success in life and work is empathy." Empathy means putting yourself in another person's situation: wondering what it would be like to be them, understanding what they are going through and supporting them.

3. Make eye contact. Rumi said that, "The light that shines in the eyes is the light of the heart." When we make eye contact we expose our heart and communicate more powerfully. I often wonder if so many of us don't make eye contact because we don't feel our heart or because we are scared to feel it.

4. Be honest, real and sincere. Like Dr. Phil says, be real. People can tell when we are not and even worse we are lying to ourselves. When you are honest and sincere you open the lines of communications that allows heart to talk to heart. You bring forth your most passionate self and your best leadership qualities. Share the truth and people will appreciate who you are, not what you are.

5. Live with passion and enthusiasm. When you live this way you will communicate your heart's energy to others and they will be drawn to your ideas, missions and dreams.

6. Read the book *Primal Leadership: Realizing the Power of Emotional Intelligence* by Daniel Goleman.

TAP INTO THE ENERGY OF LOVE

Love is patient. Love is kind. Love does not envy. Love does not boast. Love is not proud. Love is not rude. Love is not self-seeking. Love is not easily angered. Love keeps no record of wrongs. Love does not delight in evil, but rejoices in truth. Love always protects. Love always trusts. Love always hopes. Love always perseveres. Love never fails.

I CORINTHIANS 13:4-8

What would a book about energy be without talking about love? Love, after all, is the most powerful energy source in the universe. It unites and connects. It bonds each one of us to our higher power and to each other. We may feel love when we hold a newborn baby or pet a sweet dog. We may feel it while sitting in church or meditating on the beach. Love is the divine energy that is always present, waiting to flow into your life. If you have ever been in love you know the intense surge of energy that pulses through your veins and energizes you. While we know this kind of romantic love doesn't last forever, it helps us understand the power of love. Although many of us try to tap the energy of love by getting it from others, often in needy and unhealthy ways, the best way to create more love in your life is by becoming a source of love. By being a lover you will become the loved. You don't have to get love from others to feel loved. You can love yourself and know you are loved by God. Amazingly, when you don't search for love, love will find you.

Start by loving the people who are close to you. Give your family love. Then love your friends. They may need love more than you know. If you have a job, love the people you work with and watch your productivity soar. Then love the people who are hard to love. They are often the ones who need it most. It's easier to love a newborn baby or dog but loving someone who hurts or upsets you demonstrates your true capacity for love. Giving love to those who anger or upset me has been a big challenge in my life, but I find as I practice sharing my love with these people, I increase my energy and become a better person.

Just the other day I experienced the power of love in my life. My brother made a few comments that upset me on the phone. Because he is pretty closed off emotionally he makes it hard to love him. I got off the phone and was really angry. But after I cooled off, I decided to accept him for who he is. I said to myself, "I can't change him, but I can love him." So I did. A few days later, he called me up, which he hardly ever does, and underneath our conversation I could detect the love he had for me, his brother.

When we decide to become a source of love something amazing happens. Rather than trying to search for love, we start to feel it. When we feel it, we share it with others. In return we receive more love from them. This creates more energy for everyone. It all starts with the conscious decision to tap the energy of love. Here are a few Action Steps to help you become a source of love.

👟 ACTION STEPS

1. Ask four questions:

≈ How can I create more love today?
≈ How can I share more love today?
≈ How can I be open to receiving more love today?
≈ Who needs my love today?

2. Answer these questions by your actions.

SURROUND YOURSELF
WITH OTHER ENERGY
ADDICTS

When I find myself fading, I close my eyes and realize my friends are my energy.

ANONYMOUS

My dad used to say that you can tell a lot about a person by the people they surround themselves with. He was more right than he could have known. The people we surround ourselves with have the potential to give us a boost of energy or zap our energy. If you have ever had someone encourage you to "go for it" and "make it happen" or given you ideas and positive feedback, you know how we can be energized by others. On the other hand, if you have had someone tell you to "give up" and "you don't have what it takes" or made you feel inferior, you know how this can potentially fill us up with negative energy and doubts.

Who do you surround yourself with? Do they fuel you up or drain the life right out of you?

No one lives in a vacuum. We need each other. It takes more than one instrument to make a symphony and it takes more than nine players to make a baseball team. And even golf and tennis players need guidance and support from coaches. Who you surround yourself with says a lot about you and how much energy you want to have. Instead of wasting time and energy trying to convince the people who don't believe in us, we need to spend more time with the people who support us. The key is to identify these people and make time to spend with them. If they are Energy Addicts, they will be someone who wants to help you increase your energy. They will want you to be more successful. They will be a mentor. Instead of draining your energy they will want to create more energy for both of you. Here are a few Action Steps to help you surround yourself with other Energy Addicts.

 ACTION STEPS

1. Move the doubters out of your life: Make room for the Energy Addicts. In my own life, I have been doubted every step of the way and I have learned there are two kinds of people: those who are getting on our bus and those who wave as we go by. We don't have time or energy for those who don't believe in us. We have a life to live and dreams to create. We need to take the time we have and spend it with people who fuel our lives with positive energy.

2. Determine who helps you increase your energy. Who is a positive source of energy in your life?

3. Find ways to spend more time with these people. For example, make a date night each week to go out with your significant other, make Saturday night friends night out or meet a mentor for lunch or breakfast every Monday.

4. Identify five ways to energize a friend, family member, co-worker or employee. Start now and ask them to do the same.

WRITE FOR ENERGY

Writing is a great way to create and express positive energy as well as release the clutter in your mind. I recommend people keep a daily journal. Doing so helps us go within to uncover our fears, desires, thoughts and dreams—to get in touch with who we are and allow the real us to shine. Writing helps us free up emotional energy that drains us and allows new energy to flow in. When we put pen to paper we release energy from our mind and put this energy on the paper. Writing helps us project our thoughts to the world and reminds us of our wishes. I notice when I am writing I am happier, more fulfilled and easier to be around. Thankfully, my wife feels the same way. While I have written this book to help others, the ironic thing is I am helping myself. It is as if I am writing to encourage, motivate and inspire myself.

When you write, write for yourself. Don't try to write perfect grammar or even complete sentences. Just write what comes to mind and release it on paper. Don't monitor your thoughts or make judgments of whether they are good or bad. After you are done writing you can read it. Just release the clutter that has built up inside you and think of the act of writing as a healing and clearing force of energy that sweeps through you and releases everything that is holding you back. When you are done writing take a few deep breaths and let all the new positive energy flow into your life.

ACTION STEPS

1. Buy a journal at a book or card store. Or use your

computer or a pad of paper.

2. Make sure your journal is private and ask the people you live with to respect your privacy.

3. Stephen King, in his book *On Writing*, recommends we find a comfortable and quiet place to write. Even buy a writing chair. It's that important.

4. Stephen King also recommends we pick a time each day to write and make it a ritual. Make it a habit. I find I write best in the morning when I feel fresh and rested.

5. Read *The Artist's Way* by Julia Cameron and Mark Bryan. This book is one of those timeless treasures.

6. Visit Running Rhino, www.runningrhino.com, to order a journal online or call them at (206) 284-2868.

PRAY FOR GUIDANCE

*Take the first step in faith. You don't have to see the whole staircase,
just take the first step.*

DR. MARTIN LUTHER KING JR.

In the book, *The Greatest Salesman in the World,* Og Mandino writes we should pray for guidance. This simple lesson changed my life more than any lesson I have ever learned.

A few years ago I was working for a technology company. I had a feeling the company might be heading towards difficult times, like so many technology companies, so I started considering other options. Having been in the restaurant business in the past, I decided to get back into it with the hopes it would do well enough to give me the time to write, teach, speak and coach. My plan was to create an economic foundation for my family with the restaurants that would allow me to live my mission as a writer, energy coach and teacher. I franchised a restaurant called Moe's Southwest Grill and laid all the groundwork for it to open while I was working for the technology company. A week before the restaurant opened I received the call. My boss was on the other line. He said, "Hi, Jon, we need to talk." "Yes," I said. "We need to get on a call with the HR person here shortly." I was stunned as my heart began to race. "Am I being fired?" I asked thinking this couldn't be happening now. My boss was quiet for a few seconds, "Yes, Jon. You're being terminated today." It was one of the worst feelings I have ever had and if you have ever been fired you know what I mean. At first I went into panic mode. *What about my family?,* I thought. Insurance? Bills? Then I thought about the restaurant. Thank God I had put a plan in place. Thank God for the book *Who*

Moved My Cheese, which taught me to smell the cheese and smell it often. By smelling I knew my future was in doubt so I made plans. Thank God for the book *Rich Dad, Poor Dad,* that got me thinking about owning my own business to build wealth and freedom.

But then I panicked again. What if the restaurant failed? What if it didn't make money? What would I do then? All of our money was invested in the restaurant and we even took out a home equity loan to finance it. So if the restaurant went under we wouldn't be able to pay our bills and we would lose the equity in our house and our house itself. With all these thoughts running through my mind, I felt powerless. Never had I felt like this before. At that very moment I began to let go. I surrendered. I prayed for guidance. I had no choice. Everything was in God's hands.

I chose to believe I was fired at this moment for a reason and I would be provided for if I had faith. In fact, I soon realized there was a great reason for me being fired. Instead of thinking about a job I was able to pour my energy into making the restaurant successful. We opened the first week breaking even. I continued to pray for guidance. After the first month I realized I wouldn't make enough money to pay my family's bills. I continued to pray for guidance. Out of the blue I received a call from a friend who told me he had a consulting opportunity for me. It was only six weeks but they would pay me $13,000. Of course, I said. I couldn't believe it. This carried me and my family a few months. Sure enough my restaurant became wildly successful and we have been doing well ever since.

I continued to pray for guidance. I then opened two more Moe's and built a management team to run them so I could do my life's work. I prayed for guidance. I met a couple of CEOs through my restaurant and told them I also was a writer and speaker. They invited me to speak to their company and I realized the audience loved when I talked about energy. I decided to focus my writing and speaking solely on energy.

I continued to pray for guidance. I started an online

newsletter offering energy tips. Soon the list grew and grew as people e-mailed each other. One of my e-mails made it to a publisher. He thought people needed to hear what I had to say and so he decided to publish this book.

I continued to pray for guidance. Several friends told various companies about me and I was hired again and again to do seminars. I didn't even pursue seminars. They just happened. And now, I am here today helping people energize their life, making a difference, and doing what I love to do. I realize the day I was fired, I was being guided. When I let go and put my trust in God I allowed my purpose and my life to unfold. I tell this story knowing full well my life could be very different. I am very humble and thankful for the way things turned out and I say "thank you" every day.

I hope my story will help you realize when you pray for guidance you tap into your highest and higher power and greatest source of wisdom and energy. No matter what your religion may be, there is one universal source of energy that will guide you where you need to go if you ask, if you let go, if you surrender, and if let yourself be guided. The fact you are reading these words right now tells me you will soon experience this for yourself.

👟 ACTION STEPS

1. Pray for guidance. You might say, "God, please guide me on my life's path. I pray that you will guide me and help me live my purpose. Give me the strength to get through this difficult time and show me the way to my higher purpose."

OPEN YOUR CHAKRAS

Somewhere out beyond right and wrong there is a field, I'll meet you there.

RUMI

Caroline Myss, Ph.D., in her eye-opening program Energy Anatomy, discusses the Seven Chakras, or energy centers, that exist within our energy system. According to Myss, these Chakras function as central circuits or power centers that run vertically down the center of our body and manage the flow of energy through our energy system.

Whether you believe in the concept of Chakras or not, we can all agree our energetic body, with electricity coursing through our cells and organs, is affected by the flow of energy into and out of our life. When we open up we allow new energy to flow freely through our energetic mind and body without being inhibited by energetic blockages.

The way to open up is to simply be open and flexible. It sounds easy and yet so many of us are closed off to new ideas and new people that we create our own energy blocks. I have experienced this first hand. When my family and I moved to Ponte Vedra Beach from Atlanta we bought a house from a very nice couple with kids. Six months after moving in, we were outside with the kids and our neighbor came up to us and said, "I'm sorry I haven't been by to say hello. It's just that I was really close to the people who lived there before." My wife and I didn't know what to say. When we went inside, we looked at each other and wondered what being close to the people who lived there had anything to do with us. If she took the time to know us, she could become close friends with us as well. Then she would have two sets of friends—

former neighbors and current neighbors.

Unfortunately, many people go through life closed off to meeting new people, experiencing new events and learning new ideas. They hold onto the past or rigid ideas and don't allow new energy into their life. Living closed off prevents them from experiencing life to the fullest. To live a life filled with energy it is important to be open and flexible. It is essential to open your mind to new ideas, new perspectives and open your heart to new people. It is vital to expand your mind and be flexible. If an event or situation doesn't go the way you expect, be flexible. If a person doesn't act the way you want them to act, be flexible. It may be one of your life lessons and if you don't learn to be open it will keep occurring.

So the next time someone disagrees with your point of view, listen to their perspective. You don't have to agree but you will benefit by listening. If someone wants to share an idea with you, be open. It may change your business or your life. And if a new person moves in near your home, no matter how good friends you were with the people who lived there previously, go say "hello" and make more friends. The more you are open the more energy you will allow into your life.

ACTION STEPS

1. Identify if and how you are rigid, controlling and closed off.

2. Identify three to five ways that you can be more open.

3. Pick one way to open up and determine how you are going to be more open this week. For example, you may decide to be open to new ideas. This week you will listen to anyone who presents a new idea to you.

FUEL UP WITH WORDS

*One's mind, once stretched by a new idea,
never regains its original dimensions.*

OLIVER WENDELL HOLMES

I'm sure you've noticed I have included many books in the various actions steps in this book. I do so because books and words are energy that have the power to inspire, motivate and energize us. When we fuel up with the right books and the right energy we function more optimally. We raise our vibration and become more positive and live more energetically. Read a powerful book and you will never be able to look at life the same way again. Read a book that changes your perspective and you'll be forever changed. Read a book that motivates you and you'll improve the way you live. Each book you read has the potential to fuel you up with the energy you need when you need it.

The books I have listed here are just suggestions. I recommend you try them and also go to a book store and see what jumps out at you. I promise, a few books will. I love bookstores and I love books. I have heard that you really don't find books but rather the books we need find us, and I would agree. Every book I have ever read has become a part of me and my favorite books have changed who I am, what I think, and how I live my life—forever. Knowing great books have helped millions of people improve their life, I urge you to be open to the positive energy of words that will bring a greater source of energy into your life.

ACTION STEPS

1. Go to a bookstore and look around. See what jumps out at you.

2. Buy one book that appeals to you.

3. Make time each day to read it. Even 15 minutes a day will lead to a lot of books over time.

WHEN YOU'RE STRESSED, TURN ON THE LIGHT

I am not bound to win, I am bound to be true. I am not bound to succeed, but I am bound to live up to the light I have.

ABRAHAM LINCOLN

We all know what stress can do to us. When our stress rises we can literally feel the energy leak out of our body. Our mind fogs, our heart races and our body slumps. While the book *Don't Sweat the Small Stuff* offers 100 ways to keep the little things from taking over our life, I thought I would offer one way to transform any stressful situation into a positive experience. It's not something I have perfected doing, but it's something I know works when I do it. Like you, I try to improve every day.

When we are faced with a stressful situation we need to turn on the light. Just like we turned on the light to neutralize our Energy Vampires, we can turn on the light to conquer our darkest moments. Stress is a negative emotion. It is heavy energy that can weigh us down. Yet it has one weakness. Stress can not survive in the light. Nor can any negative thought, word, belief or feeling. The light is too powerful.

When facing a stressful situation, start breathing. Take several energizing breaths discussed earlier in the book. If possible, close your eyes. Focus on your breathing. Stop thinking about everything else and just focus on your breathing. Think, " breathe in, breathe out" to help you focus. After a few focused breaths start visualizing yourself as a calm and happy person while you continue your energizing breaths. Think about what you are thankful for. Think about what's good in your life. Even if you have a difficult time, something has to be good.

Then focus on the big picture. Think about your life right now and wonder in the grand scheme of things if it really is that important. Ask how important it would be if you were really sick or dying. Continue breathing and return to focusing on each breath. Imagine yourself pulling all the energy around you into your mind and body and imagine this energy giving you the strength to accomplish whatever needs to be accomplished. Open your eyes and keep the light turned on. You should feel de-stressed and reenergized.

Remember one thing. To turn on the light you must want to get rid of stress. Many of us like to tell people how stressed we are because we think it makes us appear more successful. We say things like, "I'm so busy, I'm just stressed. I have so much to do." What we are really saying is "Look at me. I'm so busy so I'm important and successful." This becomes our story, our drama, and we start identifying with it. It becomes who we are. We have to be willing to give up this mindset. We have to let go of our story and give up the drama. Once we do this we are ready to turn on the light and become energized instead of stressed.

BE AN ENERGY BANKER

As human beings, our greatness lies not so much in being able to remake the world…as in being able to remake ourselves.

MAHATMA GANDHI

An Energy Banker makes smart investments with their energy. An Energy Banker knows they have to invest upfront in order to see a return on their investment. If they sit on the sidelines they'll never create any energy.

As you apply the strategies in this book I encourage you to be an Energy Banker. Don't sit on the sidelines. Don't be scared of investing your energy in habits, beliefs, and actions that will increase your value tenfold. This is not the stock market, thank God. This is your energy. So be bold and take actions that will help you transform your potential energy into actual energy. Sure, you'll have to expend more energy upfront. Taking action requires more energy. But the energy you create as a result will far surpass any upfront investment. It doesn't take a big upfront investment either. A few simple changes and a little extra energy will provide you with big results. The more energy investments you make the higher your energy portfolio will go. Eventually energy investments and big returns will become a normal part of your life and you'll get use to operating at a higher energy level.

Every day I make two energy investments that help me live each day to the fullest. The first comes from a lesson I learned from my Cornell lacrosse coach, Richie Moran. As a freshman trying out for the varsity team, I walked into the coach's office and complained I wasn't playing well. I told him that I was better than this and that I was going to show him that I was better. I said, "Just watch over the next few weeks you'll see." He interrupted my blabbing and said something I have lived by ever since. He said, "Hey, kid, we don't talk this game, we play it. Now get out of here and do it on the field." I walked out of his office, hurt, stunned and angry. I thought he was wrong for talking to me like that. Years later I realize he couldn't have been more right. The next day I decided to stop talking and start playing. To this day I realize the talkers talk and the doers do. Each day I make the investment in being a doer and I hope you will too.

The other investment I make is in the belief that we should live 365 lives a year for the rest of our life. I described this mindset earlier in the book and I urge you to live each day to the fullest. Be a doer and do it to the fullest. Take action. Invest your energy and create more energy for your life. Create more energy for your family, your career, and your community. Apply a few or more of the strategies in this book to your life. Be an Energy Banker and become an Energy Addict.

I would like to thank you for allowing me to share my energy with you. I hope it makes a difference in your life. I wish you all the best and may your life be filled with boundless energy. Please e-mail me anytime and let me know how you are doing. jon@jongordon.com

READING LIST

Baker, Dan and Cameron Stauth. *What Happy People Know*. Emmaus, PA: Rodale, 2003.

Cailliet, Rene and Leonard Gross. *The Rejuvenation Strategy*. New York: Doubleday, 1987.

Chopra, Deepak. *Perfect Health*. New York: Three Rivers Press, 2001.

Chopra, Deepak and David Simon. *Grow Younger, Live Longer*. New York: Three Rivers Press, 2001.

Cooper, Robert. *High Energy Living*. New York: New American Library, 2002.

Dyer, Wayne. *10 Secrets for Success and Inner Peace*. Carlsbad: Hay House, 2001.

Grandjean, Etienne. *Fitting the Task to the Man: A Textbook of Occupational Ergonomics*. London: Taylor & Francis, 1988.

Mark, Vernon and Jeffrey Mark. *Brain Power: A Neurosurgeon's Complete Program to Maintain and Enhance Brain Fitness Throughout Your Life*. Boston: Houghton Mifflin, 1989.

Moore-Ede, Martin. *The Twenty-Four Hour Society*. Reading, Mass: Addison-Wesley, 1993.

Myss, Caroline. *Sacred Contracts*. New York: Harmony Books, 2001.

Rossi, Ernest Lawrence. *The 20-Minute Break*. Los Angeles: Tarcher, 1991.

Scott, Susan. *Fierce Conversations: Achieving Success at Work & in Life, One Conversation at a Time*. New York: Viking Press, 2002.

Thayer, Robert. *The Origin of Everyday Moods: Managing Energy, Tension and Stress*. New York: Oxford University Press, 1997.

Tolle, Eckhart. *The Power of Now*. Novato, CA: New World Library, 1999.

Weil, Andrew. *Eating Well for Optimum Health*. New York: Quill, 2001.

Williamson, Marianne. *Everyday Grace*. New York: Riverhead Books, 2002.